RECLAIMING YOUR FAMILY

*Seven Ways to Take Control of
What Goes on in Your Home*

RECLAIMING YOUR FAMILY

ROBERT & DEBRA BRUCE

BROADMAN
& HOLMAN
PUBLISHERS

Nashville, Tennessee

© 1994
Broadman & Holman Publishers
All rights reserved

Printed in the United States of America

4261-50
0-8054-6150-7

Dewey Decimal Classification: 306.85
Subject Heading: FAMILY \ PARENTING
Library of Congress Card Catalog Number: 94-9672

Library of Congress Cataloging-in-Publication Data

Bruce, Robert G., 1949– .
    Reclaiming your family : 7 ways to gain control of what goes on in your home / by Robert and Debra Bruce.
        p   cm.
    ISBN 0-8054-6150-7
    1. Child rearing—Religious aspects—Christianity. 2. Family—United States—Religious life. I. Bruce, Debra Fulghum, 1951– .
II. Title.

    HQ769.3.B78   1994
    649'.1—dc20
                                                                    94-9672
                                                                    CIP

To our children,
Rob, Brittnye, and Ashley,
who add wonderment to the Bruce family

Acknowledgments

With utmost appreciation to:

Roy E. and Jewel Holden Fulghum.

Rev. Mac and Lori Steinmeyer.

Janis Whipple, our enthusiastic editor who believed in the message of this book.

James A. Wessman, C.P.A., senior partner with Thomas Craig & Company of Tampa, Florida.

Angus Williams, Jr., senior agent with Principal Financial Group of Tampa, Florida.

Ellen Oldacre, editor of *ParentLife* and *Living with Teen-agers* magazines, for use of published material for this book.

Living Well Publications, Northeast Florida's health, fitness and lifestyle publication, for permission to reprint material.

Representative Tillie K. Fowler (R-Fla.), who represents Florida's 4th Congressional District, for taking the time to write the foreword for this book.

Contents

Foreword

by Representative Tillie K. Fowler of Florida's Fourth Congressional District

The twentieth century has brought many wonderful things: lifesaving medical innovations, vastly improved methods of transportation and communication, scientific breakthroughs of all kinds, and relief from much of the backbreaking labor, which used to be necessary just to survive.

In recent years, unfortunately, these advances have been accompanied by some negative developments as well, including an erosion of moral values; decreasing respect for the traditional institutions of church, home, and family; and a growing rate of crime and violence that has stressed our society almost to the breaking point.

Although many factors have contributed to these disturbing trends, there is no question that the gradual move away from traditional values and the nuclear family is a major culprit. As a nation, we have lost our perspective on what is truly important. We have become more preoccupied with material things and less concerned with intangibles like relationships and personal integrity, and our families are fast becoming casualties of our shortsightedness. What we are just beginning to realize is that the disintegration of families is inflicting devastating consequences not only upon individuals and communities, but upon our nation as well.

The family is the foundation of society; and, as any builder knows, when the integrity of the foundation is compromised the entire edifice is in danger of crumbling. As family values have declined, the rate of crime and violence has grown exponentially.

It seems frighteningly clear that we are raising a generation which is unable to tell the difference between right and wrong. With no moral compass to guide them through a growing wilderness of moral relativism, our young people are not equipped to take care of themselves, much less future generations. Make no mistake about it, this is a crisis situation that has serious implications for us all.

Even the media is beginning to realize the extent of the problem. The same reporters that ridiculed former Vice-President Dan Quayle for talking about "family values" now regularly run stories about the problems faced by unwed mothers and illegitimate babies, about boys brought up with no fathers as role models, and about children who become criminals before they are old enough to vote.

Part of the solution is realizing that in life, as in art, one of the most important elements of success is perspective. For the artist, perspective means drawing or painting to fool the eye into seeing something that is not there—distance, for example, or three dimensions instead of two. For the rest of us, it means exactly the opposite—seeing what is really there and what is truly important. Exercising perspective from a

Christian point of view, we see that our relationships with God and each other should be our top priorities.

Perspective also dictates that we take a deep breath and slow down a little. Relationships take time and for far too many of us life has become a kind of race. Rushing from activity to activity, we have little time for prayer and meditation and are constantly bombarded with information we have no time to digest. High tech, high-speed and high-pressure have replaced high quality in our lives, and many of us are left feeling out of control and wondering how to cope.

When I was growing up in Milledgeville, Georgia, the world was a very different place. In those days, it seemed as if there was always plenty of time. My brother and sisters and I had time for swimming in the lake, playing with the neighborhood children, and going to MYF meetings at the Methodist church down the block. We weren't angels by any stretch of the imagination—we also spent plenty of time squabbling about chores and homework and the other things children argue about. But the four of us knew what was expected of us and—for the most part—did it.

My parents seemed to have time, too—at least they always had time for each other and for us. My mother, who had been a school teacher, stayed home once she had children, and even though Daddy worked long hours, he put a premium on spending time with the family. The six of us ate dinner together almost every night, and we spent many evenings singing around the piano or playing cards and board games— there was a perpetual game of Monopoly set up in the den. We rarely watched television, not only because there was less programming then, but also because Mother and Daddy thought there were better things to do.

My parents were very strict, and we had some hard times too, but when I look back on my childhood, I remember one long succession of happy moments—drinking iced tea on the porch with my grandmother, parties in our basement (which was the sole domain of the children), and an endless parade of young people trooping in and out of the house at all hours.

I am sure one of the reasons my parents worked to make our house "home base" for our friends was so they could keep an eye on us, but whatever the reason, everyone loved to come to our house. To this day, many of my childhood friends go to visit my mother when they are home. Although I realize now that my parents spent a great deal of time and energy giving us the attention and supervision we needed, all we knew then was that we had a secure home and were loved, totally and unconditionally.

As adults, I think we have all tried to bring that same feeling of security to our own families. When my husband, Buck, and I started our family, we made the decision that I would stay at home. Even though I knew it was the right thing to do, I have to admit that I was initially afraid I would miss the intellectual stimulation of work, not to mention the extra income. As it turned out, I never regretted my decision. Although we did without a few things while living on only one salary, those years were some of the most enjoyable and satisfying times of my life.

Not only did spending time with my girls make me a better mother, it made me a better person as well. I tend to be rather hard-driving, especially when working, and the years I spent at home taught me some invaluable lessons in patience and perspective. In addition, I was able to contribute to the community as a volunteer, which was immensely rewarding. As Christians so often discover, what originally seems to be something of a sacrifice can, in fact, be a gift.

Those special times of my girlhood and with my own children are now more the stuff of television commercials than real life for many people. Yet what they represent—commitment to God, family, and traditional values—is something which must be reclaimed if we are to get our nation back on track. And the first step toward that goal must be taken at home, by adjusting our perspective, renewing our commitment to traditional values, and regaining control of our families.

Reclaiming Your Family is a practical how-to manual for regaining control of our families. With a strong biblical foundation, sound psychology, and a great deal of plain common sense, Robert and Debra Bruce have produced a map to help the family of today get back on the right road and stay there—together. Nothing could be more valuable.

Tillie K. Fowler, Republican congresswoman from Florida's Fourth Congressional District, is a strong advocate of family issues.

Is Your Family Out of Control?

Before our children could speak for themselves, we had heard that most children always wanted what they did not have. We honestly believed that our children would not be that way. Now, after parenting three teens, we know the true symptoms of losing control of the family while giving children "too much, too soon." But after some years of improving our parenting skills, we also have a good idea about how to treat this problem that surfaces even in the Christian home.

Take our middle daughter, for example. When she was in seventh grade, it seemed that whatever she wanted, her girl-friends already had. Brittnye wanted designer jeans; Jennifer had three pairs. Brittnye longed for her own bedroom; Carli was an only child. Brittnye yearned for boys to call each night; Alicia "went out" with a different boy each week. Brittnye's constant desire for things she did not have made life miserable for her at age thirteen and for the rest of the family as well.

Now that Brittnye is eighteen and a freshman at Emory University, we look back on the days of "I want and I have to have . . ." and laugh together. She now establishes her own goals and the trends she feels comfortable with, leaning on our family's values. She admires the clothes of others, but she takes pride in her unique wardrobe. She would like to "party" all weekend like some of her peers but "hates feeling tired and unprepared on Monday morning," she tells us as she makes curfew during summer months at home.

Getting through the peer pressure and envy that overwhelmed Brittnye in her early teen years was difficult. We listened to her whims and desires yet remained firm but kind with our family's rules and limitations.

Even the Best Families Lose Control

According to many authorities, children in America today have been given far too much, too soon, by insecure, doting parents who have "lost control" of the family. We do not mean just material items when we say too much. We also mean children being given too many choices in life by well-meaning parents—parents who care so much they would go the ends of the earth to provide for their child's wants and needs. Yes, these are parents who have lost control of their family.

This does not mean that giving to children is all wrong, for every child has basic needs that most loving parents fulfill. But giving more than a child needs or with the intention of making him or her happy for the moment or just to keep up with peers is out of line with the Christian way of life. This is also detrimental to the children as they may not be able to afford this extravagant lifestyle in adulthood, possibly leading to feelings of self-doubt in later years.

Let's look at other areas in which many families today have lost control.

Giving the Child Too Much Fun and Excitement

Children who have fun all the time begin to feel that life is simply for play and pleasure. While play is an important part of life, there comes a time when schoolwork and other less enjoyable commitments must be tackled.

"Our home is a constant celebration," says Nina (not her real name). "The kids have spend-the-nights every Friday night. Jack takes everyone out in the boat all day on Saturday; then we order pizzas for whoever stays for dinner. After that, we all stay up until past midnight watching videos on the VCR."

What Nina did not share was that her children had no home responsibilities or chores, and the family rarely made it to church, as everyone was so exhausted on Sunday morning. She also complains regularly that her children are doing poorly in school. "Maybe the teacher just isn't fun or creative enough," she rationalizes.

Children who experience life as one big party take this unrealistic attitude with them into the world when they leave home. They are the ones who suffer when they realize that not all of life is pleasure; some work is routine, mundane, and necessary.

Allowing the Child to Watch Too Much Television

Television is a natural form of entertainment for everyone. This media is probably the most important influence on child development in America today, with reports of children viewing an average of three to five hours of television daily. While the action on the screen can hold the interest of any child, does a constant diet of watching sitcoms, cartoons, and violence honestly benefit our children? Absolutely not!

Congress began worrying about the effect of TV violence forty years ago when a wave of juvenile delinquency hit our nation. Now, with violent crime increasing and out of control in most cities, Congress is worrying about TV violence once again.

Christian values are not reinforced by the media in our culture, making it impossible at times to recapture the family, especially when studies claim that many children spend more time listening to the television than to their parents or teachers. Until Congress begins regulation of television violence, parents must be the watchdog. Popular shows such as "The Simpsons," "Beavis & Butt-head," and many seemingly innocent Saturday morning cartoons are not fit for viewing by our children.

In one study conducted by several news magazines, the most obvious violence over an eighteen-hour period of TV programming was found in children's cartoons, with 471 violent acts reported. It is estimated that by the time a child finishes elementary school, he or she will have witnessed 8,000 murders and 100,000 acts of violence on television. If these statistics are not alarming enough, consider these:

➤ Five out of every six Americans will be victims of violent crime sometime during their lives, according to the U.S. Justice Department.
➤ The rate of violent crimes by juveniles increased by 27 percent in the last decade, according to FBI figures. The number of juveniles arrested for violent crimes has more than tripled since 1965.
➤ An estimated 100,000 students carry a gun to school, according to the National Education Survey.
➤ In the past seven years, the murder rate among fourteen- to seventeen-year-olds has doubled. Homicide is the leading cause of death among those between the ages of twenty and twenty-four and the second-leading cause of death among adolescents.[1]

Sherry N., a fifth grade teacher for twelve years, said, "I can tell which kids in my class watch too much television on the weekend. They seem dull and listless, as if their creative energy has been drained and not refilled. These are usually the same students who do poorly on standardized tests and have few social skills. Why should they? They have not interacted intellectually or creatively all weekend."

Watching a steady diet of television can shut down a child's creative prowess and motivation for learning, turning them into a fragmented MTV-rock video generation.

While it may seem easy to allow children to keep company with the TV, this often becomes one more stumbling block in children's maturation and development. And the messages they receive from the programs are not consistent with the message of the Christian family.

Giving the Child Too Much

Who can blame children for feeling deprived when they do not get all they want? A trip to a local mall is like stepping into a candy store with enticing window displays, the latest electronic devices, and signs that scream "Buy Me."

We know from experience that on a tiring shopping trip with three children, it is sometimes easier to just give in, allowing them to have their hearts' desire, rather than to say no.

Recently we overheard an argument between a woman and her daughter while shopping.

"Everyone wears shirts with rock groups on them," the child whined. "I'll be the biggest 'nobody' at school next week if you won't buy it for me."

The mother looked distressed, but wearily pulled out her charge card and said, "Well, if everyone has it, go on and get it."

On these shopping trips we have to ask ourselves if everyone has jeans with holes in inappropriate places, would we still want our child to wear them? Of course, we do purchase some trendy clothes and some clothes with labels if they are reasonably priced, but to make purchases because "everyone does it" is not a valid reason.

We could go on and on about the many areas in which parents overindulge their children:

➤ Too much junk food.
➤ Too little family time.
➤ Too many friends.
➤ Too little time spent "alone."
➤ Too many extracurricular activities.
➤ Too few family rules.
➤ Too little time spent at church or in family worship.

As overindulged children grow into teenagers, so do their demands: fancy cars that are given to them—no strings attached, elaborate stereo systems, the latest computer or video games, CD players, personal VCRs, no curfews, and more. Families are out of control and must stop this persistent demand for more before it ruins the family itself.

Breakdown of Families

What has happened to the family in the past three decades? In a nation where family stability was once commended, we have become a people out of control because we have neglected the family. Urie Bronfenbrenner of Cornell University said,

> We like to think of America as a child-centered society, but our actions belie our words. A hard look at our institutions and way of life reveals that our national priorities lie elsewhere. The pursuit of affluence, the worship of material things, the hard sell and the soft, the willingness to accept technology as a substitute for human relationships have brought us to the point where a broken television set or a

broken computer provokes more indignation and more action than a broken family or a broken child.[2]

President Bill Clinton, in his State of the Union Address on January 25, 1994, expressed great alarm at the breakup of the family over the past twenty years—the problem of fathers' failure to support the children they bring into this world, the severe crime problem with the rapid growth of our children turning to drugs and crime, welfare failures, the health insurance crisis with some thirty-nine million Americans without health insurance.

Blending inspiration with determination, the President challenged Americans to change, saying:

> The American people have got to want to change from within if we are going to bring back work, family, church, and community. Let's give our children a future. Let us take away their guns and give them books. Let us overcome despair and replace it with hope. Let us, by our example, teach them to obey the law, respect our neighbors, and cherish our values. Let us weave these sturdy threads into a new American community that once more can stand strong against the forces of despair and evil because everybody has a chance to walk into a better tomorrow.[3]

This book will offer ways we can all walk into a better tomorrow as we stop this persistent disease that is breaking our homes apart, which even we as Christians are not immune from. This disease is the rapid decline of the family as the foundational unit of our society or more simply put—broken families out of control. There have been problems in society throughout history, but the unique problem of our modern world is that society seems destined to destroy the very institution that could keep it strong—the family.

In the 1930s, less than 20 percent of women in the United States worked outside the home. Today over 58 percent of the mothers with children under the age of six years leave to go to work each day. [4] The traditional family concept of a dad who works outside the home and a mom who stays at home and cares for the children is the exception in today's society.

In the 1940s, divorce was not a common choice. Today, the divorce rate shows that over half of married families are split apart from reasons ranging from incompatibility and unfaithfulness to boredom and indifference. For a remarriage, statistics show that more than two out of three marriages will end in divorce.

Families today do not fall into a set stereotype. Many parents work two jobs to support their children. A typical family today could also be a single working parent, stepparents with combined families, or an extended member of the family caring for the children.

There Is Hope for the Family

But inasmuch as we might want to turn back time, that is not an option. While the traditional model has undergone a dramatic metamorphosis, this does not mean that we have to give up on family! The good news is that we can begin with the family we have, determine the true function of our family, and reclaim this intention.

No matter what the makeup of your home—a traditional family, two working parents, a single parent, stepparents, a grandparent raising grandchildren, or other—a family in control with Christ at the helm must share the same purpose: a place where love and commitment are felt among those dwelling together, goals and values are shared, and decisions are made with Christ's teachings and love in mind.

The Changing Family

Today our society is in rapid change, especially concerning the roles of men and women. This perspective has shifted tremendously since the roles dramatized by Ward and June Cleaver in the familiar sitcom "Leave It To Beaver." In a study commissioned by the Family Research Council in 1993, 72 percent of the one thousand Americans surveyed said that these changes in family life over the past three decades "have been generally for the worse." Sixty percent believe "children are generally worse off today" than when they were children, and 66 percent say "children are no longer safe at their school or at play in their neighborhood."[5]

While we may dream of that traditional family where mothers stayed home full time, this is not a realistic answer for over half of all American families today. The high cost of living dictates that in more than 50 percent of families it takes two incomes to make ends meet. For a single parent who works to support the family, the dream of having that stay-at-home mother baking cookies in the kitchen when the children come home from school is just that in most homes—a dream. Yes, changes in roles have occurred, but society must begin to accept this and support the institution of the family.

As family roles shift, we are faced with other changes in the definition of family:

➤ Dual-career families
➤ Families without children
➤ Stepparents
➤ Blended families
➤ Older parents
➤ Single parent families
➤ Scattered families with little support
➤ Caregivers substituting for parents
➤ Alternative "family" lifestyles
➤ Erosion of the nuclear family

While each of these changes may affect the meaning of "family," this does not mean that your family must fail. You can work to reclaim your family by uniting the members, assessing your family's priorities and starting with new goals and dreams, no matter what difficulties you have experienced. (See the Family Assessment Quiz at the end of this introduction.)

Yes, You Can Have Control

There are many factors families do not have control over. You may not have control over a divorce that happened in the past or the fact that both parents must work long hours to pay the rent. You certainly cannot control situations at home that have been hurtful. However, there are many aspects of family life you can control, such as:

➤ Sharing mealtime together—whether breakfast or dinner.
➤ consistently disciplining the children so they grow up understanding right and wrong.
➤ Spending time to teach family values and personal standards each day.
➤ Praying together—before school or before bedtime.
➤ Working together on family projects—helping a neighbor, visiting an invalid, writing letters to grandparents.
➤ Scheduling family night each week—a time when everyone can be together without outside interference.
➤ Limiting television time, to enjoy each other's company.
➤ Letting the children understand the family's budget and teaching them to postpone instant gratification as they save for desired items.
➤ Attending Sunday School and worship together.
➤ Spending time together each day, talking and listening.
➤ Having special times with each child alone.
➤ Playing together—a board game, sports activity, or weekend trip.
➤ Working out conflicts and disagreements creatively without screaming or arguing.

➤ Setting up family rules and curfews and following through with appropriate consequences when these standards are broken.

➤ Being there for one another when disappointment or failure occurs.

➤ Putting God and family before job or outside interests.

As the leaders of the family, you represent control. You don't have to worry what others think about the rules you have for your children. And you don't have to give in to all the latest "theories" of childrearing—diplomatic yesterday, permissive today, autocratic tomorrow, child-centered, parent-centered, me-centered, you-centered—especially in a society that does not offer much support for families after the latest theories are reported.

To reclaim your family, start right now and take pride in being unique and in being in control with appropriate rules, privileges, and consequences for your children. Parents do not have to apologize for being parents, for taking control of their children and the family. It is time for people to stop talking about the failure of the family and start boasting about the distinct attributes and strengths families can have—as they gain control of what goes on in the home.

Traits of a Healthy Family

Your interest in this book shows that you are concerned about the status and well-being of the family; family is important to you. But what about in your home? Have you lost control of your family or do you have a healthy family?

Look at fifteen traits of a healthy family and see how you measure.[6]

The Healthy Family . . .

➤ Communicates and listens.

➤ Affirms and supports one another.

> ➤ Teaches respect for others.
> ➤ Develops a sense of trust.
> ➤ Has a sense of play and humor.
> ➤ Exhibits a sense of shared responsibility.
> ➤ Teaches a sense of right and wrong.
> ➤ Has a sense of unity in which rituals and traditions abound.
> ➤ Has a balance of interaction among members.
> ➤ Has a shared religious core.
> ➤ Respects the privacy of one another.
> ➤ Values service to others.
> ➤ Fosters family table time and conversation.
> ➤ Shares leisure time.
> ➤ Admits to having and seeks help with problems.

We Must Begin to Accept Responsibility

Because of the weakness of the family, we face some major concerns—repercussions that could greatly affect our children and continue for generations. How have we failed? First, because of lack of family guidelines, we have created a society of young people who are lost and confused. These children are raised by parents who are just as lost and confused. Parents have delegated the responsibility of training their children to society, and society is not prepared to handle this grave responsibility.

Many well-meaning parents expect the schools to teach their children about sex and morals. They allow the media—television, newspaper, popular magazines, and movies—to teach them about life and love. And they expect the church to teach them Christianity, faith, and values. These same parents also wonder what happened when their children go astray, placing the blame on everyone else . . . except themselves.

Parents who want to reclaim their family must be strong and consistent. Of course, children and teens are accountable to God to obey their parents as written in Colossians 3:20. "Be obedient to your parents because it pleases the Lord," and "Honor thy father and thy mother" (Ex. 20:12). A family in control takes all members—dads, moms, sisters, and brothers—working together to function properly.

We Need to Love More

Second, many parents have failed to really love their children in the way that children need to be loved. We led a youth workshop several years ago on "God and Family." Young people ages eleven through nineteen filled out a survey that gave some insight into how parents have failed to love. According to those responding to this survey, over three-fourths of the teens disapproved of the way their parents had raised them. Their responses were frightening, and the comments are to be taken seriously.

Some responses included:

➤ "I'm going to show love for my children more and tell them that I love them every day."

➤ "I'm going to be more loving by correcting them and making strong family rules and curfews."

➤ "I'm going to hug my children more and smile a lot. I will want my kids to know that they make me happy."

➤ "I'm going to be a better role model for my children and live my Christian faith. I will go to church with them each week and talk about God in my home."

➤ "I'm going to say no to my children instead of letting them do whatever they want all the time."

➤ "I am going to know where my child is and who his friends are. If he has bad friends, I am going to intervene."

And here is possibly the most tragic response:

➤ "Everything I do seems so dumb to my parents. . . . I won't let my children go through life feeling dumb. I'm going to praise them and believe in them. I want them to feel like they are the greatest children on earth and that God loves them, and I love them, too.

When young people today tell you they *need* rules and *require* curfews and *crave* affirmation and *long for* love, it is time for adults to take notice. And recapturing the family involves this tough love at times.

When our son Rob was approaching that magic age of sixteen, we told him that there would be no driver's license unless his grades were at least a 3.0. Rob was incensed! He argued with us and became angry and frustrated at the "family rule" but without success.

Finally, instead of spending his time trying to talk us out of the rule we had made, he began to put his energy into more studying and listening at school. When he reached sixteen, he had over a 3.0 average and could get his driver's license.

Yes, Rob learned a lesson, but we discovered a lesson as well when we overheard him tell his friend: "You know, I never would have respected Mom and Dad if they hadn't followed through and made me get my grades up." Giving Rob rules and goals to shoot for let him know we did really love him, even if it was painful for a while.

Last year our daughter Ashley was grounded for not doing her chores around the house one weekend. But during the week she had shown exemplary behavior, going out of her way to be considerate and cooperative. On Thursday night, we went into Ashley's room and broke one of our parenting rules of consistent discipline, telling her that she had earned back her privileges and was free to go to a slumber party with her friends. We were astounded at her reply.

"I want to be grounded," she told us. "That makes me feel secure sometimes. I don't want to go out." Evidently she had planned to straighten up her room that weekend and work on a science project. The restriction helped her channel her energy on projects that needed to be done.

We cannot say that our children always *want* to be grounded, for that is not so! But at that time in Ashley's life, knowing that her parents cared enough to give firm limits helped her set personal guidelines and control.

We Need to Share Our Faith

Families out of control have lost touch with the least of these—their children. When was the last time you . . .

➤ Hugged your child or gave your child a gentle touch?
➤ Talked to your child, not shouted or mumbled?
➤ Listened to your child?
➤ Prayed together before meals or at night or as a family?
➤ Praised your child?
➤ Encouraged your child?
➤ Understood your child?
➤ Shared your child's joy, excitement, anticipation, worries, fears, and tears?
➤ Read to your child?
➤ Explained to your child?
➤ Shared God with your child?

This last statement is the third and largest failure of families—even Christian families—today. We have failed to tell our children about God, giving them a faith to live by as they are faced with adversity in their lives.

A story is told of a little boy who was sent to bed early one evening while his parents entertained. The young boy was very frightened, and he called for one of his parents to be with him until he could get to sleep. His mother came to him and said, "Don't be afraid. God is with you."

"Yes, I know that," the child replied, "but I want a God with *skin*."

That is who Jesus Christ is—a God with skin. As God's children and representatives in this world, we are also God with skin. Jesus made eternal truth and love come alive. He invites us to do the same in our families.

We Need to Admit We Have a Problem

As we lose control of the family, our children grow up without a sense of belonging to an intimate group. This can be seen in families where parents are no longer home at dinnertime, where school activities regularly conflict with family time, where church attendance is sporadic or often nonexistent, where parents take "separate" vacations, and where advertisements govern what we do, how we dress, and how we feel about ourselves. But life does not have to be this way; *we can change*!

Before we can heal our families, we have to admit that there is a problem and that we need help. Alcoholics Anonymous has years of success using this Christian technique of forgiveness. So let's admit it: we have lost control of the very moral foundation of our society—our family.

God's Plan for Families

After asking for forgiveness, parents must then regain control of the family by taking leadership—the leadership God intended. It has been said that parents are like stationary planets with the children being tiny satellites revolving around the parent. Your behavior dictates to the child what is acceptable in life. If you want "too much," so will your child. If you watch television all evening, the child will feel it is right to do so. If you talk about wanting a car like Jerry's, a dress like Sharon's, or a new home like your best friend's, your child will rightly assume that this is appropriate behavior. But there is more! If you ignore your spiritual life day after day, your child will probably do the same. If you never attend church, your child will imitate this when he or she is older. And if you do not talk about God helping with your daily trials, your child will not know how to do this either.

The good news is that parents who are balanced in their home and look to God for guidance will model this spiritual strength to their children. As you read this book, there are millions of families across the globe who *are* in control: parents who spend evenings talking and laughing with their children instead of being glued to the television set. There are also families where parents wake the children up for Sunday School and church each week and go with them. And there are families where the parents are not afraid to say "no" to their children as they rear them in a disciplined home with high moral standards. Yes, there are families who are *in control*, who have taken seriously the responsibility of raising children in a Christian home.

God's Order for Families

God's order for families is written in Ephesians 6:4: "Do not provoke your children to anger; but bring them up in the discipline and instruction of the Lord." Christian growth in families cannot and will not take place anywhere but in Christ's church.

Along with a real commitment to Christ's church, love and discipline are also needed in family relationships. One fourteen-year-old responded in the poll we mentioned earlier, "My dad is always too busy to talk to me during the evenings. He works every night and doesn't come home until after I go to bed. I can't remember him coming to any of my softball games or school events. I always feel worthless because I look up to him so much, and he never shows he cares. He never says he loved me." Could this be your child?

Children learn from us and from our examples. They must be instructed and loved into the ways of the Lord. And the way parents learn the ways of Jesus Christ is through the church—in worship, in Bible study groups, in Sunday School classes, and from other Christians. Are you loving your family into the ways of the Lord through regular attendance at your church, prayer time together each day, Bible study and faith discussions, and through fellowship with other Christians?

Hear the Good News!

The good news is that it is *never too late* to reclaim the family—no matter how old you are or how old your children are or how devastated your family life may be. You can begin today to ask for forgiveness, show your devotion, and reconcile any differences you may have. Because God loves us through our relationship with Jesus Christ, we are forgiven and are free to become all God intended.

While forgiving those who have hurt us may be contrary to our nature, this forgiveness that Jesus taught must take place in order for growth and reconciliation to occur in families who are out of control.

Bob tells a personal story that is dear to his heart:

> I'd like to use my life to illustrate this point. I have never really known my real mother. She left our family when we were small. We would see her from time to time, but eventually she stopped coming altogether. Several years later, we heard that she had died of complications caused by alcoholism. My two younger sisters and I had lived with our father who was devoted to us and loved us. He dedicated every spare minute to us, and you know it wasn't easy for a single parent to hold a job and raise three young children.
>
> While I was in seminary at Candler School of Theology, I did a quarter's residency as a chaplain at Emory Hospital in Atlanta. We had daily evaluation sessions, and one day we shared about the importance of family in our lives. As the discussions moved around the group, touching and moving stories were told about mothers and how important each was. When it came my turn, I had to admit that my mother did

not play a large part in my life and that I really didn't care to remember much about her.

The memories I did have were very painful to tell. One occurred when I was very young. As a preschooler, I was playing with matches in our backyard and set a vacant lot on fire. As punishment, my mother burned the ends of all my fingers with the matches until they blistered. I remembered another time when she had run away and my father had taken us with him to go find her and bring her back to the family. After he talked her into getting into the car with the family, on the way home she jumped out of the moving car. The picture of her rolling down the embankment of the two-lane highway is imprinted in my mind and is as painful as if it just happened yesterday. I remember my mother getting back in the car all scratched, bloody, and dirty, and I remember feeling so alone and frightened.

At that point in my story, some students in the group were crying, and so was I. But then I remembered something that happened when I was very young, about five years old. We were living with relatives in Indiana while my father was in school, and I remembered my mother playing the piano at a gathering. I'll never forget how everyone stood around her in awe while she played and how her long, graceful hands went up and down the keys in a melodic ecstasy. Later, when I began my musical studies at age thirteen, some of my relatives said I had inherited my musical abilities from her. I went on to receive numerous piano scholarships for college and graduated with a degree in music before going to seminary.

This didn't mean much to me, until that day in the hospital, when my superior observed the beauty of the situation. The very person who had deserted our family when we needed her, who had abused me by burning my fingers, and who had caused our family untold pain was the very one responsible for the most precious gift I had—my music.

Though my mother had passed away, I reconciled with her that cold, rainy day at Emory Hospital in Atlanta, Georgia. I learned that even as much as I wanted to forget my mother, God wanted me to forgive her and be thankful for her. In spite of the painful memories I had associated with my mother, I now acknowledge her, thank her, and love her for the gift she unknowingly shared with me—the gift of music.

It Is Time to Begin

No matter how unhappy the problems at home may be or how broken the relationships are, forgiveness and reconciliation can and must be shared in order for healing to take place. Your family may be facing marital strife, or you may be living with children and teens who are out of control; you may be suffering from apathy from a spouse, or perhaps one parent is out of work. Perhaps your family has become self-centered rather than Christ-centered. Maybe your children turn on the television and turn you off, or you have so many bills that your paycheck does not make a dent. Whatever the problems your family is facing, healing can and will take place if Jesus Christ is allowed to come into your home and sit at the head of your table.

For children, parents are "God with skin." As you show love and discipline, share your faith, and say no at times, you can allow the ever-present love of Jesus Christ to shine through you and become known to your children. Children are also "God with skin" as they love, honor, and obey their parents in a manner consistent with biblical teachings.

America is ripe for family values. There is no time better than right now to reclaim your family and gain control of what goes on in your home. As you read the chapters in this book, you can begin this process if every day you . . .

➤ Pray to God about your family's needs and listen to the response.

➤ Ask for forgiveness from the hurts and wounds of the past.

➤ Invite our Lord and Savior Jesus Christ to enter into the very heart of your home and give you comfort, strength, and new enthusiasm for your family.

The blessings you will receive as a strong Christ-centered family will continue for generations to come. Yes, it is time to come home again to family!

Notes

1. "Attuned to Violence," *Florida Times-Union* Jacksonville, Florida, E-1, E-6.

2. Dr. Donald Joy, "Surrogate Relationships," *The Asbury Herald* 104: 3 (Summer 1993), 4.

3. President Bill Clinton, "State of the Union Address," as reported in the *Tampa Tribune* (January 26, 1994), A-1.

4. Quoted by Barry Bearak, "Searching for the South of a Decade," *The Los Angeles Times* (December 18, 1989), A-15.

5. "Most Americans Believe Family is Eroding, Not Merely Changing," *Florida Citizen* (February 1994), 2.

6. Dolores Curran, "What Good Families Are Doing Right," *McCall's* (March 1983), 89.

FAMILY ASSESSMENT QUIZ

The following family assessment quiz may help you evaluate the status of your family. Answer the statements on a scale of one to five, with one being of least importance and five of the greatest importance. After completion, add up your score according to the instructions that follow.

<u>Least</u>   <u>Greatest</u>
1 2 3 4 5

_____ 1. We limit watching television to one hour each night.

_____ 2. We try to have one meal a day together as a family.

_____ 3. We pray together as a family.

_____ 4. Our family attends Sunday School and church together on a regular basis.

_____ 5. One or both parents are at home with the children most nights supervising chores and homework.

_____ 6. One or both parents attend school functions, including open houses and conferences.

_____ 7. We have established family traditions in our home.

_____ 8. Each member assists with home chores.

_____ 9. Family expenses and budget are discussed openly.

_____ 10. The family's rules and the consequences for not following them are understood by all members.

_____ 11. Discipline and expectations are consistent.

_____ 12. Family trips and outings are important to us.

_____ 13. Our extended family—grandparents, aunts, uncles, etc.—is important to us.

_____ 14. When family members have problems, we talk them out openly or seek professional help.

_____ 15. Children do not have a choice in their religious upbringing.

_____ 16. Moral expectations of family members are high.

_____ 17. Homework, school projects, and reading come before television.

_____ 18. Television shows are monitored by the parents.

_____ 19. Sensitive subjects are discussed openly so children can know the facts and the parents' values.

_____ 20. Parents are always aware of who the child is with and where the child will be.

_____ 21. We allow for diversity within our home, as long as it is within family rules and values.

Count the number of 5 answers, 4 answers, and so on, and tally the results. How do you rate?

Mostly 5: Congratulations! You're on track with your family life; keep reading for added information on reclaiming your family.

Mostly 4: You are almost there. Use this source as a positive way to bring family members together.

Mostly 3: Not bad, but you might need some improvement. Check the chapters for areas to work on.

Mostly 1 & 2: Come on! Make family a priority. Take some time today to regroup as you get your home in order.

Chapter 1

Take Control Through Faith in Jesus Christ

Parenting experts through the years have recommended different focuses for successful family relationships. Some authorities have felt that the home should be child-centered, with every action geared for the well-being of the children. Other experts have claimed that the parent-centered home is most effective, with the marriage as the most important factor. This method is based on a belief that if the parents are happy and secure, the children will also be contented. While either of these focuses can work, depending on the family, to reclaim the family we must become Christ-centered in our homes. The family that is centered in Christ will consider the well-being of both the child and the parents; "others" will become the primary issue instead of "self."

Having a Christ-centered family begins as a Christian couple lets God unify the marriage relationship so they can pass on to the children a spiritual heritage. As the Scripture,

"For where two or three are gathered together in My name, there am I in their midst" (Matt. 18:20) becomes a reality in the home, children learn to seek God for guidance, comfort, and strength in their family, school, and work experiences.

Consider this statement issued by the trustees of Harvard College shortly after its founding in 1636: "Let every student be plainly instructed and earnestly pressed to consider well [that the] main end of his life and studies is to know God and Jesus Christ . . . therefore to lay Christ . . . as the only foundation of all sound knowledge and learning."

Whether or not Harvard College has lived up to its original vision remains to be seen. Yet men and women can have impeccable academic credentials, live in the finest neighborhoods, and drive expensive cars—and still be empty shells with no real purpose in life. With all their advantages they may live only for themselves and have no concept of having a relationship with God and others. Sadly this is an apt description of a large segment of our society today.

Consider Kim (not her real name) for example. This young woman seemed to have it all—a beautiful lakeside home, two healthy children, and a loving husband. Yet several months ago when Kim came to the door with red, swollen eyes, we knew something was wrong.

"We're missing something in our lives," Kim shared as she wept gently. "All these years we have taken pride in giving our sons every opportunity—sports teams, the best private school, music lessons, summer camp and more. But somehow, our relationship as a family is very empty."

Though a parent usually knows a child needs love, attention, education, or discipline, thousands of parents across the globe ignore the most important ingredient in a child's life— the importance of religious faith. In our busy family, we can understand the natural inclination to give children all of the opportunities in life so that they will become successful young adults. Yet in the midst of these advantages, researchers say that today's child is lacking a vital ingredient: a purpose or meaning in life, something to believe in and live for. In fact, studies say that children need a moral purpose in life as much or even more than they need food, clothing, and a good education. And this sense of morality does not usually come from outside the home, rather it comes from parents who serve as role models.

The Bible Gives Self-Esteem

As we reclaim the family, our goal as Christian parents is to nurture the children so they might experience God's love, with a personal faith in Jesus Christ as the expected result. This personal faith gives children a sense of belonging, for the Bible teaches the child that he or she is of ultimate worth. Christianity gives children self-esteem; they become sensitized to the perils of humanity and can respond with empathy to injustice in the world. The idea that "I am loved, therefore I can love others" is the outcome of our faith in Jesus Christ.

At a parenting workshop, Elizabeth, mother of fifteen-year-old Samuel, said, "Some friends were telling me how they had worked seven days a week for years to save enough money to give their son so he could start a business upon graduation from college. I, too, have worked seven days a week for years, but for a different purpose. I feel the greatest gift I can give to my son upon graduation is a firm foundation in the Christian faith and belief in Jesus Christ. I've worked to give Samuel a good education and a strong faith in God, and I know he will make it in this hurried world."

What Is Faith?

Faith in God through Jesus Christ gives meaning to our lives; it gives guidelines for what is significant in life and what is not as important. It is that one ingredient that allows us to wake up each morning no matter what the trials were the day before and carry on with our lives knowing that God is with us. Faith means commitment, trust, and caring for others; it enables us to risk sharing our lives with others in meaningful relationships. Because of faith that is nurtured in a caring Christian home, new lives are constantly being changed. And faith in a living Lord gives empty, lonely lives new meaning and purpose.

But this undivided faith that we speak of does not just happen. Parents must understand that faith is an ongoing process. Theologians realize that just as people mature and grow in stages, so do we develop in stages with our faith, especially as our faith matures. Religious educators have found that just as a baby crawls before he walks and then develops physically and mentally in sequence, so does our faith in God.

In the book *Will Our Children Have Faith?*, theologian and author John Westerhoff III suggests four stages in the development of faith:[1]

1. **Experienced Faith.** In this beginning stage, the person believes only what is experienced. Other people are observed and copied. This experience stage is highlighted by action and reaction towards others and events.

2. **Affiliative Faith.** The person moves into affiliating with significant persons and events. Affiliative faith involves belonging to a group, participation, and a feeling of being a part of something important.

3. **Searching Faith.** The person begins to use his or her mind to make critical judgments, including questioning and doubting. The person also begins to experiment with alternative courses of action.

4. **Owned Faith.** This is the ultimate ideal. Faith is truly "owned." The person feels the need to witness and to behave with an integrity which supports what is believed.

As parents, we can enable our children to move through the stages of faith as we make Christian education a priority in our family.

Families Build a Platform of Faith

According to Rev. Mac Steinmeyer, pastor of Killearn Lakes United Methodist Church in Tallahassee, Florida, families must develop a platform of faith in order to give children the utmost advantage in life.

"Children must have a platform of faith to build upon, to rebel against, to jump off of, and to come back to," Reverend Steinmeyer said. "This platform is so important because our children always have it no matter what life stage they are in. Without this religious foundation, children are left drifting with no purpose in life. The problem arises when some parents say they want to let children form their own faith without parental influence. They have basically provided their young with nothing spiritual to lean on or come back to in times of trials or temptation."

The raising of children is the most challenging task that God gives to human beings. But every parent needs to know that *no child is prepared for life who has not been taught the selfless love of Jesus Christ.* The greatest need our children have is to learn about the agape love that Jesus taught. If they know this love, we will not have to worry that they will be dragged down by temptation and despair later in their lives. Even in the midst of trials and tribulation, our children can always lean on that personal experience with God through Jesus Christ— their strong and secure platform of faith.

This is why the church is so important in the life of a family as children receive training in the Christian faith. Parents must take their child's attendance at church on Sunday morning just as seriously as their attendance at school.

For a discussion about "Should I Make Them Go to Church?" see chapter 2.

Worship Is a Spiritual Discipline

The idea of worshiping in the local church as a spiritual discipline has its reasoning as well. Studies show that children who stay with the local church through ninth grade may break away during college or early career, but most will come back when their own children are young. As we look around in our congregation, we can see the young adults with babies and toddlers, coming back into the fold of the church as they begin to take seriously the responsibility of raising a family in a Christian home. And many of these young adults were active in churches across the nation when they were young. Some admittedly did break away and question their faith during college and early career, but they are now back and actively joining committees, Sunday School classes, and study groups, while enrolling their infants in the nursery.

There are more reasons why we believe in the local church for our family. We have found that commitment to a congregation, a specific body of believers, is vital to complete and complement our development as Christians. Membership in a local church means being accountable to serve on committees, finding our talents and using them to help others, and developing commitment as we attend faithfully as a family.

Studying the Scriptures with a caring teacher in Sunday School and during the weekday programs and Bible studies of the church gives all of us insight into life. Through the Bible and the experiences of the pastors and teachers, we are able to understand each other and find suggestions for living a more Christ-like life. The beauty of searching God's Word within the fellowship of the church is that other caring Christians, not just Mom and Dad, are able to share how Christ has revealed Himself in their lives. Our children can learn from the experience of young Christians around them and can relate to the afflictions others have gone through.

Attending church regularly provides the family with a base of support in difficult times. Christian friends have shown us love and compassion as we experienced turning points in our life, and joy is expressed as we encounter success.

Going to worship as a family has added strength to our children as they develop their values and personal convictions. "I'm going to raise my children just like I was brought up," our daughter Brittnye said after taking communion one Sunday. The intimacy of being a close family unit taking communion together was important to her; it was an experience that she wanted to repeat again with her children.

Learning from Our Christian Heritage

While church attendance is important to families, regular attendance at church is not enough for children to understand their faith and its importance in their lives. How can one or two hours a week compensate for the other influences in today's society? A Gallup poll on religion in the home found that 75 percent of parents questioned said that the home (compared to church or school) is the most important in religious training of children.[2] In order to relay a living faith in the family, parents must build on that Christian heritage and talk to their children about God, and they must do so every chance they have.

Consider how families were centered in the early part of this century. Instead of children being alone in empty homes during afternoon hours glued to the TV, they spent their free time close by their parents, siblings, and extended family, helping with chores or even working in the fields. Evenings were not spent with video games, the telephone, or the television set, but they were spent reading books, talking to other family members, or going to church services.

In the early days of this country, authority was deeply embedded in social functions of church, family, and neighborhood. Sociologist Robert A. Nesbit observed that this authority was so closely woven into the fabric of tradition and morality as to be scarcely noticeable.[3] With such a family-oriented society, the negative influences of society were not nearly as intense as today.

The American family today is being reconfigured, however, and its role is becoming much more complex. Previously, families were expected to focus solely on the physical survival of their members. Now they are expected to provide a great deal of the emotional and social support as well.

What many people do not realize is that families have life cycles and stages, just as do the individuals within it. Some periods are more stressful than others; such as times of illness, divorce, death, or economic crisis; the addition of a stepparent or siblings; or a grandparent coming to live with the family.[4]

We cannot turn back the clock and imitate the family lifestyle of our ancestors, but we can certainly learn from the past. We can observe history and see how people received power for living through the various life cycles and stages of the family. What gave them hope? How were they able to continue in the midst of adversity? Where did they turn when faced with hunger, sickness, or death? How did they keep their family loyal and connected? Our ancestors received this power by being strongly rooted in family values and a belief in a living God. We can recapture these roots. As parents we should ask ourselves: "Are we building on that strength by laying the same religious foundation and family roots for our children?"

Our model is the same one our ancestors had, the charge given in Deuteronomy 11:18–21, 26–28.

You shall therefore lay up these words of mine in your heart and in your soul; and you shall bind them as a sign upon your hand, and they shall be as frontlet between your eyes. And you shall teach them to your children, talking of them when you are sitting in your house, and when you are walking by the way, and when you lie down and when you rise. And you shall write them upon the doorposts of your house and upon your gates, that your days and the days of your children may be multiplied in the land. (RSV)

How to Share Your Faith

There are many ways for parents to introduce their children to a living faith in God through day-to-day experiences. Many Christian parents believe that daily rituals in the home are the key to encouraging a strong foundation of faith.

Make a Personal Commitment to Christ

A child's spirituality depends on the parent understanding and interpreting the Christian faith from a personal viewpoint. First, you must begin with yourself. Have you made a commitment to Christ? Consider the statements on what it means to be born again, listed below.

Before you can relay a living faith to your children as they grow spiritually in the family, you must understand God's plan for salvation. Look over the following true statements and see how they relate to your spiritual knowledge and commitment.

1. "For all have sinned and come short of the glory of God" (Rom. 3:23, KJV). Everyone is a sinner; there are no exceptions.

2. "For the wages of sin is death; but the gift of God is eternal life through Jesus Christ our Lord" (Rom. 6:23, KJV). Death means separation forever from God and from His love through Jesus Christ.

3. "But God commendeth his love toward us, in that, while we were yet sinners, Christ died for us" (Rom. 5:8, KJV). God loves us so much that He gave His son to die for our sins.

4. "If thou shalt confess with thy mouth the Lord Jesus, and shalt believe in thine heart that God hath raised him from the dead, thou shalt be saved" (Rom. 10:9, KJV). To be born again, you must believe the Jesus died for your sins and state publicly that you accept Him as Lord of your life.

5. "For whosoever shall call upon the name of the Lord shall be saved" (Rom.10:13, KJV). This is God's promise to you: if you accept Jesus as Lord, He will accept you.[5]

After you have studied these Scriptures, contemplate how God through Jesus Christ is part of your daily living. If you have further questions regarding salvation and your faith, contact a pastor or a Christian friend. If you have never made a life commitment to Jesus Christ, perhaps you might do so right now. Ask for God through Jesus Christ to come into your life and guide your family, using this prayer of salvation:

"Lord Jesus Christ,
I trust you as my Savior and my Lord.
Forgive my sins and come into my life right now.
Help me to live daily for you.
Amen."

Live Your Commitment

Greater than anything you can ever say, your actions will let others know about your faith in Christ. If you are loving, compassionate, and honest, your child will emulate this in his or her life. Your child will also watch as you are benevolent toward others, turn the other cheek when challenged at work, or stand up for your Christian beliefs in the community.

The Bible says, "Do not let the sun go down on your anger" (Eph. 4:26). Families who live their Christian commitment take to heart Bible verses such as this and let these words guide their daily living. The biblical accounts, stories, illustrations, and helps are the perfect rule book for governing the family—if we only take these to heart and allow God's Word to guide our daily actions in the home.

A friend shared, "When I was growing up, my mother took care of her great aunt in our home as we were the only family she had. Aunt Veronica was elderly and was bedridden due to a stroke. As my mother made her comfortable, took her meals, and read her stories out of the Bible, she would include me. 'You need to learn this,' she would say to me. Today, I am caring for my husband's mother in our home. I am so thankful that my mother not only lived compassion, but took time to teach me the ways of family and love."

Talk with Your Children About God

After attending church with his family for sixteen years, Joey asked his father one day, "Dad, are you a Christian?" To which his father replied, "Of course I am! Don't you know that I go to church each week and teach Sunday School?"

Young Joey looked at his father very intently and said, "But, Dad, you have never told me about God."

How many of us are guilty of going through the motions each week—taking our children to church, singing in the choir, leading studies and classes, ushering, chairing church committees—but never actually telling how God has made a difference in our personal lives?

Children can see the strength that an intimate commitment in Christ can give when their parents take time each day to talk about this.

Tell your children how Jesus has made a difference in your life. Tell them about the power of prayer and give examples of when God answered a specific prayer for you. Talk about salvation, forgiveness, and the personal strength only Jesus Christ can give. Teach them about your denomination and its beliefs, the sacraments, and the liturgy. Show them Scriptures that describe God's love, and lead them to a saving knowledge of our Lord. Faith in God will become a reality if you spend time passing on this heritage at home.

A three-year-old boy in our church playschool asked his mother where Jesus lived. She replied, "That is kind of hard to say, because it isn't some place you can get to by car or plane. You can't even take a space shuttle to heaven." The young boy continued to ask questions about where Jesus lived, until she finally said, "Sweetheart, I can't tell you exactly where heaven is, but I do know that it is a beautiful place where both God and Jesus live."

Her son's face then lit up and his eyes glowed as he said, "That's wonderful! Because my Sunday School teacher told me that Jesus is right here in my heart. That must be the beautiful place where heaven is."

That true example makes it clear that there is a blessing when we, like the Hebrews of old, answer our children's questions about their faith and constantly talk about the symbols and beliefs. The young mother took time to honestly explain about heaven, and the small child interpreted this in terms he could relate to.

Be a Confident Witness

In Mark 5:19, we read, "Go home to your family and tell them how much the Lord has done for you and how he has had mercy on you" (NIV). What can your family members do to become more confident in witnessing of their Christian faith? Let's look at the following ways.

Develop a Daily Devotion Habit

In 1882, on the campus of Cambridge University, the world was first given the slogan: "Remember the morning watch."

Students like Hooper and Thornton found their days filled with studies, lectures, games, and bull sessions. However, these dedicated men soon discovered a flaw in their spiritual armor—a small crack, which if not soon closed, would bring disaster.

They sought an answer and came up with a scheme they called the "morning watch"—a plan to spend the first minutes of the new day alone with God, praying and reading the Bible. The morning watch sealed the crack. It enshrined a truth so often obscured by the pressure of ceaseless activity that it needs daily rediscovery: To know God, it is necessary to spend consistent time with Him.[6]

Through daily quiet time and meditation, we all can realize a more personal faith with God through Jesus Christ. During this devotion period, we can gain an understanding of ourselves that is vital in order to share the faith that truly touches our souls. Devotional time and prayer continue the ongoing personal relationship between God and self, and these times of meditation and aloneness allow us to learn who we are, as well as whose we are.

Our youngest daughter Ashley was once overheard talking to a friend: "Every morning when I get ready for school, I see my dad in the living room reading the Bible and taking notes. I guess it means a lot to him to do this."

Plan for a devotional time in your life, and talk with your children about why you do this. Children will imitate what they see parents doing in the home.

Join a Church and Attend Regularly—Together

In order for parents to reclaim a Christ-centered family, church membership and attendance is necessary. One of the best witnessing opportunities we have is to let our children know that going to church each week is important to us. Can you imagine expecting your child to have a personal relationship with Jesus Christ when you sleep in or play golf every

Sunday morning? This is no different from expecting the child to make high scores in math without making him go to school each day. To learn about Jesus Christ, families must go to the place where teachers and preachers are telling the Good News—the local church.

"Going to church gives our family a ceremonious and organized way of proclaiming our faith in Jesus," said Katherine, a mother of two teenagers. "As we sit in church as a family, we are forced to let all of our problems go and focus on God. This time each week helps us realize what is important in life, no matter what the weeks' troubles were. And we always leave feeling uplifted, with new hope for the week."

Going to church should begin at the youngest age. We are learning now that even very young children have religious experiences; they just cannot put the experiences into words so that we are aware of them. As church nursery workers hold an infant in their arms, they lay the foundation for the faith of that child by giving an experience of love and acceptance within the family of faith.[7]

Churches have ongoing programs, classes, prayer groups, and more that can meet all your family's inner spiritual needs. Find out what is available at your church—Bible and book studies, small groups for all ages, children's and youth choirs, youth meetings, women's groups, men's studies, family suppers and more—and see how this can meet the needs of your family members.

If you are not a member of a church, find one with a creative Sunday School program, a solid music program for all ages, and an active youth group. Then make it a habit to take your family each week. If you are a member of a church that is not meeting your family's needs, don't just quit! Help to build a strong children's and youth ministry and become part of the solution in your church to make changes for the good of all families. Get involved, make suggestions for improvement, and take leadership positions. Remember, the church is the people, and each member is vital to its function in the community.

A Witness Needs Knowledge

"Go therefore and make disciples of all nations . . . " (Matt. 28:19–20). Fulfilling Jesus' commandment begins with our personal experience, belief, and witness. But without knowledge of His Word, we are unable to be effective witnesses.

Allow God to speak to you through His Word and really listen. How many times do we all read the Bible without hearing words for our life! Open your heart and mind as you prepare for God to touch your life in a meaningful way.

Parents should lead the way as they study the Bible, both privately and with others. The Bible provides inspiration, strength, knowledge, and insight into human living and can give a strong background to every Christian who is striving for a deeper faith.

Josh tells of reading Bible stories to his five-year-old son every night. "I have done this since he was a toddler," he said. "The stories are very interesting, but more importantly, I think the habit of turning to the Bible each evening will stay with him when he is old enough to do this himself."

Take turns sharing favorite Bible verses with family members as you discuss the importance of turning to God's Word for knowledge and strength. Have the Bible prominently displayed in your home so your children and their friends will know it is important to you and your family. And let your children see you reading the Bible throughout the day.

Make sure that your child has his or her own Bible, and encourage your child to circle or underline favorite verses. The Bible must be worn—marked, written in, used, highlighted—to be effective in the life of the reader. Georgianna Summers in *Teaching as Jesus Taught* suggests that we place an exclamation mark (!) for ideas that we find exciting, a question mark (?) for ideas that need clarification, an upward arrow (▲) for that which seems to tell us, "Do this," and a downward arrow (▼) for the message "Stop doing this."[8]

Witness from the Eyes of Your Soul

Many parents ask "What exactly do I say to my child when I find that perfect time to witness to my faith?" The best way to explain the Gospel to others is to simply tell them what you believe or what you have experienced in your life. You simply relate your Christian encounters to others by sharing your life. As Jesus said, " . . . You are witnesses of these things" (Luke 24:45–49).

Witnessing to your child about the importance of God in your life can take place each day as you take time to share your faith. Look at the following statements and see how they show your child that you hold God's love in highest esteem.

➤ "This rose bud makes me feel so hopeful, just as God gives us hope each day to begin anew."
➤ "Let's pray that Sammy's father will find a job. I know God will take care of them."
➤ "Mrs. Johnson has been ill. Let's make some cookies and take them to her to show God's love."
➤ "I always get goosebumps when I watch a sunset. It reminds me of God's awesome power in our lives."
➤ "Sometimes you have to ignore what people say. God wants us to be bigger people and turn the other cheek."
➤ "I forgive you for doing that. Isn't it wonderful that we can be forgiven and start over as God forgives us?"
➤ "Sometimes we don't know why things happen as they do. That's what faith is all about; it's trusting that God will do what is best for us."

Live Your Faith

Lori, mother of seven-year-old Jordan, feels the best way to talk about her faith in a manner that he can understand is to explain benevolent actions. "On Christmas Eve I volunteered to help serve one hundred dialysis patients at a local clinic in our town. I took Jordan with me and, as we served the plates, I explained to him how important it was to help others. He helped me hold the plates and beamed as the patients took their dinners.

"We have also sorted Jordan's toys for a local shelter for abused children in our city, and talked about giving to those who are needy," Lori continued. "I feel that this is part of God's plan—for the strong to care for the weak—and we have involved him in these actions."

Dan, the father of three boys, said, "I feel that you can encourage your family members to begin to share their faith at home, in a safe environment with people they know. Have your children tell about nonverbal ways they can let others know they are Christians. In our home we affirm such actions as giving a hug to someone who is hurting, doing a kind deed, writing a note to a lonely friend, or making a phone call to someone who is ill."

Think about your actions each day, and try to make them relate God so your children will understand His love and power. John 15:11 teaches us, "These things I have spoken to you, that My joy may be in you, and that your joy may be made full."

Discuss the meaning of faith with your family. Faith means commitment, trust, caring for others. Faith enables us to risk sharing our lives with others in meaningful relationships. Because of faith that is nurtured in a caring Christian home, lives are changed. And faith in a living Lord gives empty, lonely lives new meaning and purpose.

Start Family Rituals

As you discover the importance of faith for your family, consider the importance of family religious rituals. Rituals provide family identity, which fosters self-esteem in adolescence. They show children that they belong and are important. If they feel good about themselves in the family, they are less likely to act out together.[9]

Prayer is one ritual in our home that we join together for day after day. At dinnertime each evening, all members of the family join hands and offer to God prayers of thanksgiving for the day. At times when our children were preteens this religious ritual embarrassed them, especially when their friends came over for dinner. But we have persisted with this and now as older teens and young adults, they are the first to grab their sibling's or parent's hand as an expression of love and unity. The embarrassment is gone, and the tradition of family prayer is established—one they will take with them to their families in later years.

Other religious rituals families have include reading the Bible together at a certain time, having a devotion time each morning before school and work, keeping prayer lists for members to pray for each other, or memorizing helpful Scriptures. Find a ritual that suits your family's stage and needs, and do this habitually. Realize that these times will not always be perfect; if your family is like ours, there will usually be someone out-of-sorts at times. But repetition is necessary in order for meaningful, shared experiences to happen. Your children will begin to look forward to this "habit" as it becomes a regular part of their lives. In later years, this family ritual will become something held in highest esteem—something that belongs to your family.

Plan a Regular Family Devotional

Another ritual we have celebrated as our children developed is a regular devotional together as a family. This time was scheduled, specifically set aside to allow members to slow down and come together as a family. The devotions included times of singing together and talking about God; it was a time where we were able to establish our roots deeper in the Christian faith.

Select a Topic for Sharing

As you make plans for family devotions, ask yourself, What issues concern my children? You may choose a broad topic to discuss, such as love, faith, friends, or caring. Or you may want to narrow your sharing time to a specific concern, such as family love, brotherly love, or loving the unlovely.

Sadie said she found active listening important in selecting a topic for her three boys during their weekly sharing time. She said: "I try to hear what the children are really saying and use these messages to plan devotions for the next time. For example, last week my fourteen-year-old son told us how he had become disillusioned with the media. He realized that several published stories about crime in the schools were richly embellished, and he did not like that. Our sharing time the next Sunday night dealt with the issue of truth and how Christians are called to be truthful in all walks of life. If we don't teach them a Christian viewpoint, where will they learn this?"

Another mother of two girls discovered that gossip was an issue with her daughters. "My eleven-year-old told us how friends at school had been dividing up into two cliques. Then a few weeks ago, one group started spreading rumors about the other and vice versa. She was torn between the groups, as she had friends in each. We talked about the repercussions of gossip as a family, and some personal sharing supported by Scriptures and wisdom helped her work through this."

Support with Scripture References

Using a reference guide such as a topical concordance, look under the topic you will be talking about with your family. The subject guide will list topics from anger, affirmation, and affliction to topics like tenderness, tension, and thanksgiving. Under each topic a list of related texts can be found. The various texts under a single topic offer excellent material for family sharing times and prayer. Suggested headings may stimulate new ideas for your family. And many topics give related ideas you can research for more scriptural background.

Include Personal Testimony

Be sure to support your Scripture verse with a personal testimony. The most convincing examples are those you have experienced. Perhaps God became real to you through a mistake or failure. Do not tell the story with the intention of glorifying yourself, however; look for anecdotes in your life that will glorify God.

You may also find a poem, quote, or story to be helpful in stimulating sharing with your children. Inspirational books such as *Leaves of Gold* by Clyde F. Lytle and any of Helen Steiner Rice's collections are helpful. Other resources for story-related statements that speak to children and youth include *Love Is a Magic Penny* by Tom Neufer Emswiler and *Pungent Prayers* edited by Philip E. Pierce.

If you are going to share a personal testimony with your family, try to keep it brief, to the point, and related to the ages at your home. A two-minute devotional can touch more young lives than a lengthy, involved dissertation.

Celebrate with a Song

Music has always been important in our home. Our devotional times are full of singing and playing musical instruments. Singing during the family sharing time helps to break down barriers that may create tension among the members. Not only does the music relax the soul, but the words have an important message that will be imprinted on the minds of the young.

Find a song that may relate in some way to your family sharing time. If you are talking about love, the traditional hymn "Love Lifted Me" or the favorite "Jesus Loves Me" may be appropriate for your children. You may choose to be more contemporary and select a song by Christian musicians like Amy Grant, Sandy Patti, and Michael W. Smith.

Hugh enjoys playing piano with his children during family devotions and talks about the good times they celebrate together: "Once a week, usually Saturday evening after dinner, we talk about things that went on during the week, have a family prayer, then I play some of the favorite hymns and songs for the kids. Even our teenage son hangs around for this special time before going out with his friends. It is 'our' time, and we protect this as being important in our home."

Close with a Personal Message and Prayer

Offer a time where your children can relate their lives to the topic being discussed and add personal insights to the Scripture passage. In our family, we have used this time for affirming one another, asking for forgiveness, or voicing a personal concern or prayer need. The moment is intimate and the atmosphere is one of concern, which helps the members feel comfortable in sharing their deepest thoughts.

Making the Scripture come to life in your home means involvement and a response from each member. A personal sharing and prayer time allows for this response to take place. The prayer does not have to be lengthy and can be as simple as "Thank you, God." You may choose to have your family join hands and close with a conversational prayer, where each member prays a sentence prayer aloud. Or you may choose to say the Lord's Prayer in unison.

Remember to . . .

➤ Provide an environment where grace can be experienced in your devotional time. This involves smooth transition between family discussion, sharing of personal concerns, and prayer. An environment of grace requires that the parents be caring and help the children feel love and concern for one another.

➤ Avoid appearing too pious or self-righteous during the devotion time. It is important that you be approachable as you lead the children. If your faith appears real to your children, they will model this in their lives.

➤ Talk in a language your children can understand. The Bible instructs us to come like a child to the Father (see Luke 18:17). Our prayers and words with children and teens need to be simple and easy to comprehend. Family members can thus learn that God is loving, caring, and understanding like a parent or a friend. We should all respect God's awesome power yet also trust God enough to want to share our everyday concerns.

➤ Encourage your children to continue having personal devotional times in their own lives. You may make the suggested resources available for each child. Suggest to them Scriptures they can study to continue the devotion topic. Encourage listening to God. Often we become so involved with pouring out our troubles and woes that we forget to listen for answers. Train your children to take time to be still and hear God speak.

Sharing times in your family can be one of the most exciting adventures parents and children can participate in. A meaningful sharing time begins with loving parents who care enough to plan and who provide a rich environment in the home where God's grace can be shared.

Teaching Children to Pray

Maxie Dunnam describes the human need for prayer saying, "As living beings, we breathe, we eat, we drink, we sleep. As human beings, we breathe, eat, drink, sleep, and pray. It's a part of our nature as human beings to pray." [10]

Most Christian parents want their children to have a personal relationship with God. This awareness that God knows them, cares about them, and has a plan for their lives can be a reality as you take time to teach your child to pray.

Make Plans to Be Together

A Saturday afternoon spent out-of-doors with your child is the perfect time to begin this teaching. You can sit on a blanket under a shade tree in your backyard, take a picnic supper to a nearby park, or go anywhere that is conducive to being at one with God and for personal sharing.

Set the Mood

If your children are like ours, they are not always going to be in a frame of mind to talk about something as personal as their prayer life. Many children often do not feel like praying or do not think they need to pray. To some older children or teens, praying aloud or even admitting that they pray is embarrassing. You may have to wait for signals from them, such as questions they have regarding God and prayer, disappointments or sadness they are faced with, unanswered prayers or answers to prayer they didn't expect.

Choose a time when your child is in a congenial mood, then suggest that he spend some quiet time out-of-doors with you. Ann said that she always looks for that moment when her teenage daughter is feeling low and hanging around more than usual. "I know that when Casey is quiet and not as rambunctious as usual, she needs time for prayer and support from my husband Tom or me."

Begin with the Bible

As you give your child suggestions for praying, begin with the Bible. Here we find Scriptures encouraging us to pray, teaching us how to pray, providing examples of prayer, and giving us answers to our prayers. In Mark 11:24, we read, "Therefore, I tell you, whatever you ask in prayer, believe that you have received it, and it will be yours" (RSV).

With the Bible as your guide, look at the following precepts as you train your children to develop their prayer life with their Heavenly Father.

Speak in a Child's Language

Teach your child that talking to God is like talking to a dear friend. Most children regard God as a parental figure. If a child has experienced strong parental love, he or she is able to see God as being strong like a father and gentle like a mother. Explain that God is all-caring and wants to know your child's innermost thoughts, fears, and dreams. Tell your child he or she does not have to use impressive words to get God's attention; sincere words are much more important. Abstract terms only add to the confusion and mystery of our faith. Let your child know he can keep prayer at a conversational level, expressing needs to God as he talks with Him.

Encourage Sharing During the Prayer Time

Let your child know that God wants to know all about the concerns, needs, and problems your child may have in his or her life. Personal joys can include answers to prayers, goals met, or relationships that have been enhanced. Concerns include praying for those who are ill, personal stumbling blocks, or unresolved conflict with friends.

Often children have a difficult time expressing their feelings openly with God. You can help your child learn to do this by giving him some open-ended sentences and asking him to fill in the blanks silently. For example,

> ➤ I am happy about _____.
> ➤ I am thankful for _____.

➤ I am sad about_____.
➤ I worry about_____.
➤ I want to pray for_____.
➤ I am afraid of _____.
➤ I want God to heal_____.
➤ At school, I need prayer for_____.
➤ I want God to bless _____.

As you give your child suggestions for filling in the blanks, he can begin to establish communication with God that will enhance his personal devotion life.

Talk About Answers to Prayer

One of the most difficult tasks that parents face is helping their children cope with situations that do not seem fair. From praying for health and not getting well instantly, to praying to win the Student Council election and losing, children can feel the disappointment of what they believe is unanswered prayer.

As you talk with your child about prayer, you must continually emphasize that God loves us, and He understands when we are sad. Acknowledge that you do not have all the answers saying, "I don't know why, but I do know God loves us and wants the best for us."

Let your child know that God answers prayers in many ways. He may say "yes," "no," "maybe," "wait," or "I'm going to surprise you."

"Yes" is the obvious answer we all want to hear when we pray. But you can talk with your child about other answers God gives. While we should pray for what we want, we must realize that God knows us better than we know ourselves, and He knows what is best for our life.

Look at the following statements. Ask your child which statements he or she believes to be true about prayer, and use the answers to discuss what prayer really is.

➤ God never hears my prayers.
➤ God hears my prayers and answers them.
➤ I only pray when I want something.
➤ I only pray when I am sad or frightened.
➤ Some things are too unimportant to bother God with.
➤ God doesn't always answer my prayers.
➤ God doesn't always hear what I am saying.
➤ I shouldn't have to pray if God knows all.

Children must be taught that everything—the good and the bad—is important to God, and He hears and answers all prayers. God wants us to pray because it establishes a relationship with Him, just as our friends need us to talk with them. Let your child know that even though God's answers to our prayers may differ from our expectations, we are to bring everything in prayer to our Father in Heaven.

Explain the Different Aspects of Prayer

You can explain different prayer "formulas" that can help your child get focused as he prays. We have found the formula entitled ACTS to be helpful in our family. This acronym speaks of the different ingredients of prayer which are adoration or praise, confession and asking for forgiveness, thanksgiving, and supplication or petitions for self and others. Ask your child to think of specific prayers in each category:

➤ Adoration (praising God): _____
➤ Confession (of wrong behavior and sins): _____
➤ Thanksgiving: _____
➤ Petitions (for self and others): _____

Some parents like to teach their children to use an other "formula" called JOY. This breaks prayer down into praying to Jesus, praying for Others, then praying for Yourself. Talk with your child about these methods of praying and see if they may help him get started.

Start a Family Prayer List

Compile a family prayer list where members can list specific needs or requests, and family members can lift these up in personal devotion time. Hang this prayer list up in the kitchen so all can see, and write in cross answers to prayer as they occur.

Encourage your child to see prayer as more than a series of requests but as a way of life, a oneness with our Heavenly Father. The ultimate purpose you can role model for your child is to treat prayer as ongoing communication, as you talk of God's love and try to structure your actions to be like His. Your child will learn that prayer is not just a two-minute activity, but a day-in and day-out relationship with a loving Father.

Pray Without Ceasing

Encourage your child to "pray without ceasing" (1 Thess. 5:17) with these suggestions:

➤ Spontaneous prayers throughout the day can help your child recognize the love of God in his life.
➤ A simple song can be a powerful prayer if the attitude is right.
➤ A poem or Scripture describing feelings on a specific topic can be read by your child.
➤ A one sentence, "Thank you, God," can be said at anytime.

Talk About Eternal Life

Is it not interesting how surprised we are when death occurs to a friend or loved one? Most of us live as if we are going to be healthy and alive forever. But the reality of life is that all of us are going to die.

Christians believe that death is moving from life on earth to another life—an eternal one. Facing death as part of life and sharing the burden of sorrow along with the hope of eternal life is vital teaching for our children. But this teaching needs to be shared in the context of the Christian faith with the promises it holds.

It is sad that death in our society has become so sterile and institutionalized, so far removed from the course of everyday events. Not too long ago most people died at home, and families were involved in the process all along. But with medical advances in recent years, then with life-saving procedures and equipment ever on the increase, the death process has become increasingly an institutional one. What this has done is to shelter and to hide the reality of death from our children. It is not uncommon for persons to be well into their adult years and still have never attended a funeral or seen a dead person.

Our culture seems adamant on trying to hide the fact that death is part of life. We hide the sick and the infirm away in hospitals and nursing homes, and when death comes, it is often behind closed doors with no close relatives around. Sometimes even the rituals of funerals seem to shelter us from the reality of death, and we are content to have it that way.

It is never easy to accept death. When a loved one dies, adults and children alike may feel angry, confused, or emotionally numb. We may not know how to express our feelings of loss or how to say goodbye to the person who has died. But facing death as part of life and sharing the burden of sorrow— along with the hope of eternal life—is important for our children if this teaching is shared in the context of the Christian faith with the promises it holds. This is where the family's values comes to play.

First, face the reality of death in your family. Get it straight in your mind that death is going to come into your life. Acknowledge the fact that you, too, will one day be leaving this life for the next. Therefore, live the very best you can now, in order that you will have no regrets when the end comes.

Let your children know that death is a reality for all people, and encourage them to live so that each day counts.

Second, take your child to funerals. Funerals are a positive force in the grieving process and can be helpful. Since death is not easy for anyone to face or to accept, funerals can help us to work through our feelings. A funeral is a ritual that can help focus our emotions and bring meaning to the experience of death. Rituals link us with the past and the future. We have rituals for graduations and marriages, and we need a ritual for this most important passage of life.

The funeral serves as a means to commemorate the deceased, but just as importantly, it helps the survivors to heal emotionally. When someone we love dies, we experience the pain of grief. Even though it hurts, grief is not something to avoid. This is important for our children to learn—we must not avoid grief. Grief, in fact, is the very part of the healing process that allows us to separate ourselves from the deceased person and go on with our lives.

Funerals give people a "permission" to express their feelings of sadness and loss. Funerals also stimulate them to begin talking about the deceased, one of the first steps toward accepting death. In fact, people who do not attend the funeral of a loved one because they want to deny the death may suffer from unresolved grief several months later.

To resolve their grief, people need to accept the reality of death not only on an intellectual level, but on an emotional one as well. For this reason, funerals in our culture are usually preceded by an open-casket visitation period. Research has found that the viewing of the deceased person can help you to accept the death of that person. It helps with grieving, because it shows that there is no return to this life, for death is final.

Death is an unavoidable reality, but parents can give their children the strength of our faith so it is not a crippling experience.

Third, realizing that death is a vital part of living allows the child to face life victoriously. He or she should love others for the moment instead of waiting to share his or her feelings or concern. As you explain the Christian's perspective of death to your child, remember that each child is different in his or her interpretation and response to the subject of death depending on personal experiences, knowledge, and maturity level. Emphasize the teachings of Jesus Christ and God's Word. Share the reality of the Christian faith, that God gives us strength and courage in times of darkness and sustains us even when we are at the lowest points. Teach your children that eternal life is promised for all believers. If you are confident in what you believe, you will radiate truth and surety to your children as you discuss death in your family.

Fourth, give your child straightforward answers. Closed doors, whispering, and sending the child off to a neighbor's house when there is a death in the family only adds to that child's fear of the unknown. Conversation about a pet or plant that has died will enable the child to discuss concerns and feelings. Also sharing memories of loved ones who have died can open up conversations about death. This enables your child to reaffirm that people will live on in our minds.

The Challenge Is Ours

Ground your family in the Christian faith for it is the basis for a Christ-centered life. Teach your children about God, read the Bible together, show them how to pray, and explain a Christian's perspective on eternal life. Let your children see you reading the Bible and praying with your spouse; take your children to church, and sit together as a family. Talk about how God is more than just a word in your life as you begin to share a personal faith in Jesus Christ, you're taking the first step to reclaiming your family.

Family Time

1. Ask each family member to write down character traits they need to effectively share God with others—traits like being honest, caring, listening, active, strong, and courageous. Discuss how these attributes help to build confidence as they share their faith. Encourage the use of these attributes as they tell others about God's love.

2. Ask your child, if he could pray for two things, what would he say? Help your child express himself in a manner that is comfortable, genuine, and appropriate. Talk with him about his prayer until he feels comfortable in saying the words aloud. You might start by repeating a sentence such as, "Dear God, please help my grandmother to get well," and have your child repeat this after you. Once a child becomes accustomed to praying, he or she will do this without your initiation.

Notes

1. John R. Westerhoff, III, *Will Our Children Have Faith?* (Minneapolis: The Seabury Press, l976).

2. "New Gallup Poll: Religion at Home," *Tampa Tribune*, (March 31, 1979), 5.

3. Velma C. Roof, "Social Systems and Family Life." *The Catholic World* (July-Aug, 1993), 149.

4. "What Makes Families Happy and Stable?" *USA Today* (April 1993), 8.

5. *Living with Teenagers* (Fall 1993), 25.

6. Robert D. Foster, *Seven Minutes with God* (Colorado Springs: Navpress),1.

7. Delia Touchton Halverson, *Helping Your Teen Develop Faith* (Valley Forge: Judson Press, 1988),7.

8. Georgianna Summers, *Teaching as Jesus Taught* (Nashville: Discipleship Resources, 1983), 49.

9. *Better Families,* 17:11 (November, 1993).

10. Maxie Dunnam, *The Workbook of Living Prayer* (Nashville: Upper Room, 1975), 12.

Chapter 2

Take Control Through Consistent Discipline

The lack of parental discipline is a hot topic for discussion in the world today. A recent article in the Journal of the American Academy of Pediatrics found parents guilty of lack of discipline as they failed to enforce, "consistent, age-appropriate limits" on their young. A national survey by Louis Harris & Associates revealed that 64 percent of those polled say parents just don't do a good job disciplining their children.[1]

In mountains of magazine articles and self-help books, parenting experts give advice on how to set limits and enforce these with methods from behavior modification to time-out to issuing firm consequences. Some professionals believe in permissive parenting, while others tout the benefits of being firm and strict. But so much of this secular advice is theoretical and, quite honestly, does not always seem to work when it is supposed to. Where do parents turn as we work to recapture the family?

First, parents must realize that no family is perfect. Parents may be firm disciplinarians one day, then lax the next. In our home we can go for weeks being consistent, then added work stress for both of us may make us too tired to discipline. Knowing that we are not perfect, we can still make great strides in becoming stronger disciplinarians as we renew our commitment to the family and to God's challenge as parents.

Ask any parent what is the one thing they dislike about parenting, and most will agree—discipline. But discipline is a positive word, not something you should dread. Think of where the world would be today without rules and discipline! Everyone would be doing whatever felt good at the moment without any consideration of others. The world depends on rules and consequences to function. To gain rightful control of the family as you establish yourself as the "head" of the home, discipline is the key. Balanced with loving-kindness, your firm discipline will enable your children to grow and develop into responsible, compassionate young adults.

A father of three told us with a regretful tone, "Yes, sometimes I do have to put my children in their room for time-out, but I try to avoid this because they get so angry."

Why do we try to avoid disciplining our children? Because they might not like us for the moment? Perhaps they may tell their friends or teachers that "my parents grounded me" or "my parents made me stay in my room last night." Are we so insecure that we must have everyone's approval at all times?

At a meeting in a local church, parents were asked, "If you had to do it again, what would you change about raising your children?" The responses were phenomenal:

➤ "I'd be tougher. I was afraid of my child when he was younger, and now he doesn't respect me as he should. I would be firm and in control."

➤ "I would not give in as much. I feel as if there is always pressure to do what the other parents allow for their teen.

I would stick with rules that were appropriate for our family."

➤ "I would not be so concerned about what others think when I grounded my daughter or made her do family activities instead of going off with peers. I would think first of our family and what is right for us."

➤ "I would not feel so guilty all the time for disciplining my sons. I realize that this is my duty to be in control of my family, and I wouldn't care what others thought as I raised my children in a disciplined manner."

While we obviously cannot turn back the clock and recapture what is past, we can begin today—right now—to raise our children or teens in a disciplined family using common sense to guide our actions as we lean on biblical premises for parents.

Our Biblical Challenge

Discipline comes from a word that has the same Latin root as *disciple,* which means to "teach and guide." Christian parents can turn to the Bible for direction in how to teach their children and guide their family. Although we have a biblical mandate to take control with effective discipline, too often well-meaning Christians pull from the Scriptures just those verses that empower them in life, such as the Beatitudes or Ten Commandments. Many of us have ignored the very passages that require us to discipline our children and be in control in our family. Given the powerful challenge we have to be leaders and teachers in the home, we cannot disregard the wealth of knowledge and guidelines found in the Bible any more.

Scriptures such as, "Train up a child in the way he should go; even when he is old he will not depart from it" (Prov. 22:6) require parents to take the lead in the family. The exciting news about this Scripture is that if we do follow its directive to teach and instruct our children, we have hope that they will not stray from this discipline when they are old. In a time when many children are growing up without strong family values, that is good news!

In the Great Commandment, we find the commission to "Love the Lord your God with all your heart, soul, and mind . . . . Love your neighbor as much as you love yourself" (Matt. 22:37–39, TLB). These verses focus on a discipline we all must have, for we are held accountable for our behavior, our actions, and our thoughts. Again, this one principle must be taught to our children as we hold them responsible for their behavior.

Discipline: A Twenty-four-Hour-a-Day Word

Sadly enough for many tired parents, the truth is that *discipline never ends.* Each day a parent must begin anew and start with a fresh slate. This new beginning requires two important actions from the parent—to forgive and to forget. We must forgive any opposing behavior from the child, and we must forget the negative feelings and actions from the previous day.

But what happens when a parent is overly tired or too busy with an important project when the child breaks the rules? Are we not all guilty of ignoring bad behavior at times? Look at the excuses some of the best parents give when children break family rules:

> ➤ "I just can't deal with one more thing tonight."
> ➤ "Maybe if I ignore her, she will quit."
> ➤ "She already came out of her room? Oh, well. I'll try again next time."
> ➤ "My turn to discipline him? I'm just too tired."
> ➤ "I'm just going to let them do what they want this weekend. I need a break from parenting."

➤ "Putting him in his room never works. Why try?"
➤ "She was so horrible yesterday that I don't even want to see her."
➤ "Discipline him? Why should I? It hasn't worked yet."
➤ "I don't care anymore."

Expect the Best from Your Child—Today

To be effective, discipline must address improper behavior the moment it happens—not hours later or tomorrow or next week. And this immediate reaction to your child's action is not easy! Disciplining children and recapturing the family takes work—every day and every night—as you expect responsible behavior from your child and follow through with action until he or she understands.

Especially when you have more than one child, the weariness from effective parenting takes its toll. It seems as soon as you get one child through an unpleasant rebellious stage, the next child dives in, exhibiting negative and trying behavior. Rarely does the conscientious parent get a reprieve from keeping children on the right path—and we speak from twenty years of nonstop experience! In our home it seems as if that point in time when the oldest passes through a stage, the middle child hits it head-on. When this child mellows out and begins to accept the rules, the youngest child tests the limits. One might assume that it would become easier to raise children as you gain this experience, but each child demonstrates independence and rebellion to parental rules in different ways. Whereas one child might have been vocal and outwardly rebellious, another child may be more passive in how she rebels against family rules. Just as each child is different, so are the methods we must use to train them.

As demanding as it is for the parent and as unpleasant as it might seem for the child, discipline is not an option as you reclaim your family. Although the discipline habit is tough, the benefits are great as your firm discipline will some day become your child's self-discipline. In other words, as you make your child follow family rules, stay within limits, and then administer appropriate consequences when he or she falls out of line, the child will be the winner. The child will learn how to function successfully in a society that mandates that people follow rules and stay within limits and then administers tough consequences should anyone break these laws.

Our son Rob has always been the opinionated child. Needless to say, he was the one child in our home who needed the most discipline, the firmest rules, and the strictest limits. Most of the time while growing up he had an answer for everything we told him, and according to him, his way was much better. Until . . . he went off to college. Last year Rob became a "surrogate parent" to forty freshman boys as a resident advisor in his dorm at Emory at Oxford, his "home away from home."

Reading the letters he sent, we were astounded at how much Rob began to sound like his parents. "I will *not* put up with any noise in the hallway after 11 P.M.," he wrote one week. "They can close their doors and study, or they will not be here next semester." In another letter he wrote, "When will they ever listen to me? I tell them they'd better stay on top of their grades, and they act as if everything is fine. Yet I never see them studying."

All the years of lecturing and sometimes arguing with our son paid off; he has become one of us. As he took charge of the lives of others, the discipline we gave at home became his self-discipline.

But What If My Kids Do Not Like Me?

We will never forget one young couple with four children we met at a church-related parenting workshop. Before the parent session began, the four children were running wildly around the room in an active game of chase. The mother tried her best to get control, saying softly, "Now come back here. Please, dear, stop running." And the father did contribute a little, reaching out to grab one of the children but missing as the child darted to the back of the social hall.

Later at the workshop session, we realized why the parents were unable to control their children. When we were talking about being firm and setting limits, the mother spoke openly and said, "The thought of my children not liking me for any length of time makes me so miserable. I would rather the children be happy and always love us than give them strict limits and punishment. I don't want to risk losing their love."

A most important truth as you reclaim your family is this: Parenting is not about being popular nor is it about being well-liked by your children! As you issue rules and consequences, your children will naturally be angry with you. Who wants to obey a rule when it is more fun to do what you want in life? But the love and respect you will have as a parent who cares enough to be firm far exceeds any "like" or "popularity" you may have when you are permissive.

The manner in which you discipline your child will come back to you years down the road. As you work hard to instill responsible behavior in your child with consistent discipline, they *will* one day thank you and affirm their love for you, probably when they, too, have children to discipline.

Is It Too Late to Begin?

It is never too late to start being authoritative with your discipline in the Christian home. One man came up to us after a parenting workshop and said, "Everything you talk about in raising children is the opposite of what I have done. Now I have three teenagers who don't respect me or anyone else. Is it too late to start over?"

While it is easier and more effective to begin being authoritative in the home while children are very young, it is never too late to take charge of your family. Being firm with older children and teenagers after raising them with permissive parenting techniques will be disturbing at first. Your children may openly resent you taking an active part in their life, especially if they have done as they pleased for years. But you can recapture the family with authoritative discipline if you stick with it and do not give up.

One friend, Sally, who raised two children as a single parent for years, decided when her boys were preteens that she wanted to change her method of discipline in the home. "For years the boys honestly did as they pleased," she said. "But they were good kids, so I never had any real trouble. But as they approach the teen years, I see signs of lack of respect for me and my rules. I know I have to crack down now or the teen years are going to be difficult."

Sally began using contracts with the boys and discussed these at family meetings on Friday nights. At first the boys resented the new rules and regulations of living in a family, but after awhile they adjusted and held open discussions about the fairness of the rules and the consequences when these were not upheld.

"It took about six months of adversity before the boys finally began to act like they were part of the team," she continued. "But the results are astounding. They come home after school and immediately do their homework instead of playing video games for hours. When I get home from work, they have the table set. And they respect me. We're in this together, and now we have more order in our lives."

If you have been too lenient with your children, begin with the family meeting described later in this chapter. Let your children know that the rules are changing a bit as you take control of the family. Then be prepared to have a few upheavals in family harmony as you lay down new ground rules and consequences. Whatever you do, once you have made up your mind to be authoritative in the home, do not stop. Remember that you are the parent, the adult role model for your children. Do not let your family down by weakening the authority God intends for you to have.

Each Child Is Unique

Most of us agree that authoritative discipline is vital in creating a positive, self-confident child. But one question comes to mind when applying the Scripture to "Train up a child in the way he should go; even when he is old he will not depart from it" (Prov. 22:6): Did God really create all His children to go the same way?

Charles Swindoll and others have suggested that in the original Hebrew the intent of this passage is to train up a child "according to his or her bent." The root word has to do with the bent of a tree. For instance, a willow tree that leans out over a pond toward the southern sun is bent in a certain way. If you try to force it to bend another way, you will break it.[2]

Becoming a positive parent involves nurturing each child in the family in a manner that "follows his bent," realizing the special gifts and talents God has given each one. Our "bent" is what makes life so diverse and interesting.

Look at the following statements most of us have used in moments of despair or debate with our children. Are we not comparing them with other children or with our adult "standards of excellence?"

- ➤ "How can you always be so sloppy?"
- ➤ "You act like such a baby sometimes."
- ➤ "What did I ever do to deserve a child like you?"
- ➤ "When are you ever going to get your act together and grow up?"
- ➤ "I don't think you will ever do well in school."
- ➤ "Hold your shoulders back. Your bad posture makes you look sloppy."

And the irony is that often the adults are guilty of the same charges! But these negative statements can have a disasterous impact on a child's self-esteem.

Feeling good about ourselves is becoming rare, especially in a world where daily situations tear down our self-esteem. Remember the neighbor who yelled at you when you stepped on her freshly cut lawn? Or the manager of the restaurant who angrily confronted you when your child spilled his drink on the customers at the next table?

As difficult as it is for a mature adult to maintain a positive attitude and self-image, imagine how much more difficult it is for a young, developing child! Yet the Bible affirms the unique preciousness of each child. "Then some children were brought to Him so that he might lay his hands on them and pray; and the disciples rebuked them. But Jesus said, "Let the children alone, and do not hinder them from coming to me; for the kingdom of heaven belongs to such as these" (Matt. 19:13–14). The psalmist also exalts the child saying, "Behold, children are a gift of the LORD" (Ps. 127:3).

What you say and how you act toward your child has a tremendous influence on his life and on developing self-esteem. Your thoughts, feelings, and behavior mirror your soul. If you are full of depressing thoughts, doubts, and suspicions regarding your child, then his attitude toward life will be negative. But if you are enthusiastic, hopeful, and positive, your parenting skills can be filled with meaning. Your actions and words can have a vibrant impression on your children, especially as you raise the child in the unique manner in which God intended.

Learn the Rules

The first rule of parenting is that good parents—those who have control in the family—are made, not born. While some people may have innate parenting skills and know how to lead the family, most caring parents realize it takes reading, praying, and talking to other parents to learn how to tackle this job responsibly.

If rearing a child in a Christian home using biblical guidelines is our goal, perhaps the following suggestions could help create an atmosphere of love, discipline, and respect.

Be Authoritative

In Ephesians 6:1–2 (TLB) we find, "Children, obey your parents; this is the right thing to do because he has placed them in authority over you. Honor your father and mother." This Scripture gives the ultimate standard for the behavior of a child, with obedience and respect being vital attributes the child must have. But the Scripture also gives a forthright directive for parents—to be authoritative or the expert in the family—"because he has placed them in authority over you."

The word *authority* has a negative meaning for many people, especially when it comes to raising children. At a recent seminar, one father could not handle this leadership responsibility saying, "Can't we be democratic in the family, with everyone having their say, and vote on this?" Another mother seeking help with a troubled teen said, "I just want to be his mother, not be his boss." Yet being authoritative in the family is consistent with being the expert—the one who knows. And for the Christian family, being authoritative means being a loving expert. Parents convey trust and confidence to their children when they take the role of authority, thus giving security and strength to the family unit.

Behind the parenting concerns over doing the "right" thing is a long-running scientific debate. Several recently completed studies that tracked more than one hundred children for nearly twenty years have provided the first, objective test of which disciplinary styles work best, and all point in the same direction. Parents who are not harshly punitive, but who set firm boundaries and stick to them, are significantly more likely to produce children who are high achievers and get along well with others. [3]

According to Ron Taffel, Ph.D., director of Family and Couples Treatment, Institute for Contemporary Psychotherapy in New York City, many parents want an opposite-from-my-parent approach that they are still miffed when they are less effective than their parents were. "When my mom or dad told me to do something, I did it! But my kids won't listen." Why is this so? In our zeal to not repeat the past, modern parents are often susceptible to an overdeveloped sense of fairness. As a consequence, we try so hard not to be authoritarian that we lose the ability to be authoritative. There is a big difference: Authoritative means being expert, having the ability to influence and lead—attributes kids need and respect. Authoritarian parents are unbending, rigid—they allow their children to have no say, and kids rebel. [4]

A set of longitudinal studies conducted by psychologist Diana Baumrind of the University of California at Berkeley's Institute of Human Development affirms the need to be authoritative. "Authoritarian" parents ("Do it because I'm the parent") were more likely to have discontented children. "Permissive" parents ("Do whatever you want") had children who were the least self-reliant and curious about the world, and who took the fewest risks. "Authoritative" parents ("Do it for this reason") were more likely to have self-reliant, self-controlled, contented children.[5]

While fairness is important in being authoritative, parents cannot always guarantee that the rules and answers they give to their children will sound fair. Sometimes we cannot honestly explain why a child must or must not do something. In our home, we often admit that "because it is in your best interest" or "because that's the way it is" when we can not explain the reason. An internal "gut" instinct is often what parents must follow as they issue rules and limitations. Remember, it is far better to be authoritative and risk seeming unfair at times, than to risk raising children who do not respect adults or rules. Your authority will give security to your family as you raise children who are responsible and confident.

Be Firm, But Kind

In Ephesians 6:4, Paul warns Christian parents: "And now a word to you parents. Don't keep on scolding and nagging your children, making them angry and resentful. Rather, bring them up with the loving discipline the Lord himself approves, with suggestions and godly advice" (TLB).

Parenting is about relationships—loving relationships. In order for you to discipline your child effectively, you must spend time with your child and get to know him or her. If your parent-child relationship is devoted and respectful, your discipline will be tolerated more than if a child resents you as a dictator. Before you state the punishment when rules are broken, consider these questions:

➢ Does the punishment fit the crime?
➢ Was the punishment given in a fit of anger, or was it well thought out?
➢ Is the punishment age-appropriate?
➢ Will you follow through with the punishment?
➢ Can the child grow through the punishment and learn from his or her mistakes?

Punishment for breaking family rules is not about being cruel to a child nor is it about making life miserable for the parents. It is about teaching children to follow rules and staying within these limits. Weigh this when you administer consequences to your child, and determine if the punishment will help the child learn and grow or if it will add to his or her negative attitude.

Be Reasonable

We have been guilty of telling our children, "You cannot talk on the phone for two weeks" or "You cannot go anywhere for one month" only to give in after a few days because the consequence was punishing us more than the child. Weigh the punishment to make sure you can stick firmly with it. The whole point is that your child must learn—enough to change his or her behavior.

As you administer punishment that fits the crime, make sure that it is fair and quick. It is far better to make the punishment instantaneous and to the point than to be so extreme that you do not follow through. Here are some guidelines:

➤ Be clear about what the punishment entails.
➤ Be clear about how long the punishment will last.
➤ Be clear about what you expect the punishment to accomplish.

For example, you could communicate these three aspects of punishment in this manner:

➤ "You will not have television for your punishment."
➤ "Beginning now, this punishment will last two days and two nights."
➤ "I hope you know that I mean it when I ask you to watch your sister from now on."

Give the Child Definite Limits

Children need specific limitations to have disciplined behavior. This structure will take many forms as a child grows up. The limits set for a four-year-old will certainly broaden as the child approaches fourteen. But at any age, everyone—children and adults—needs limits to survive in an ordered society.

Children should know when it is bedtime. They should have a bedtime ritual each evening of bathing and brushing their teeth, saying their prayers, and a bedtime story with Mom or Dad. Kids need to know that breakfast is served each morning at a certain time and that they must take their plate to the sink after they eat. They need to know that homework is their job each day and that if they use a bath towel, they must hang it up. Family members need to understand that prayer, Bible study, and attending church is part of your Christian lifestyle, and this spiritual ritual is expected in the family. You see, inasmuch as these limits seem restricting to a child, structure in the home offers security, because the child knows what to expect and what is expected of him or her. When families stay on a firm routine, many discipline problems are alleviated as the child understands his or her responsibilities in the home.

At a recent slumber party at our home, the girls finished their showers, leaving the bathroom a disaster area. While all the girls were in the kitchen baking cookies, one young guest quietly went in and picked up all the towels in the bathroom, meticulously hanging each over the shower door, and then wiped off the countertop. "We always do this in my family," I heard her tell another girl. What was seen as a forbidden chore for some children was an expected family routine for this child. Her parents' discipline had paid off.

Be Consistent

The greatest key to effective discipline as you reclaim the family involves being consistent in what you tell your child and reinforcing this behavior over and over again. This does not mean that you must always be right. It does mean that both parents must agree and join together to administer discipline and rules.

We came from very different family backgrounds. Bob was raised by his father who was a single parent for many years.

His grandmother, who lived with the family, had a great influence in his discipline and upbringing. My [Debra's] family was a two-parent family, yet for many childhood years, my father traveled a great deal on business and was only home on weekends, so my mother was the strong disciplinarian. Bob and I came into our marriage with different backgrounds and varying opinions about how to raise responsible children.

We have learned that rather than argue about which parenting style or method of discipline is right or wrong, it is important for us to agree on what is proper for our family and respect each other in this process. Yes, even in our family, one parent is more lenient and one parent is strict, but when we combine our ideas and opinions, and then agree upon the proper rules and discipline, the result is an atmosphere of mutual respect and firm expectations for our children. We come across to Rob, Brittnye, and Ashley as authoritative— the united front—as we work in our family with shared, acceptable rules and firm consequences.

As parents are consistent in their childrearing responsibilities, both parents must take the role of being both the "good guy" and the "bad guy." Paul and Laura, parents of three elementary-aged children, realized this after Laura was seen as the "great monster" by their children, and Paul was admired as the "wonderful king" when he came home.

"We found that Laura was doing all the disciplining each day, and I would come home and be the 'good times' daddy," Paul admitted. "Our children began to seek me out during the evening hours to get out of chores or other responsibilities that Laura gave. We realized that our kids needed to see that both parents cared enough to set limits and rules."

After some difficult evenings, both parents issued responsibilities and deadlines to the children. "They were shocked when good 'ole Dad began to require them to do the dishes each night, and Mom fixed cookies and milk before bedtime," Laura said. "But after a few days, the kids realized that Paul and I were in this together—a parenting team. They quit fighting both of us."

Teamwork with both parents involved is mandatory as you stand strong in your demands and in your support for the children. This teamwork involves some homework "behind the scenes" so that when you are faced with childhood rebellion, you are in one accord.

Single Parent Families

Single parents have the biggest challenge of all as they raise children without the support of a spouse. Mothers and fathers who are single must look to extended family members, church friends, and parent support groups (see related information in chapter 3) as they gain confidence in being authoritative in the home. When the parent is exhausted after a day at work and comes home to carpools, cleaning, homework, broken rules and dinner preparation, it is especially difficult to follow through and be consistent with discipline. This is where techniques such as family meetings and contracts become very important as child and parent join forces to take control at home.

Set Logical Consequences

Logical consequences that "fit the crime" are very effective in getting the message across to children. Bev, the mother of nine-year-old Cameron, said, "It's really important that you try not to overreact when you punish the child."

"Last week Cam broke a favorite vase with his football in my living room after I had asked him to go outside," Bev shared. "I did two things: I made him replace my vase, and I took his football away for the weekend. Of course, I gave him some extra chores so he could earn the money, but, more importantly, I wanted him to learn the value of someone's property and how he had to follow family rules."

Taking the consequences for one's actions is a wonderful lesson in life that must be learned at an early age. Sometimes these consequences are not even given by the parent (see chart below).

Behavior: A child who fools around at night and does not complete homework . . .
Consequence: Gets in trouble with teacher or receives poor grade.

Behavior: A child who forgets to bring his books home during exam week . . .
Consequence: Does poorly on tests.

Behavior: A child who ignores chores for the week . . .
Consequence: Has no privileges on the weekend.

Behavior: A child who does not eat dinner . . .
Consequence: Has an empty stomach at bedtime.

Behavior: A child who leaves toys thrown around the house or on the lawn . . .
Consequence: Has nothing to play with that week.

Sometimes it is best to let our children learn from their mistakes. Often significant character development results when the parent allows the logical consequences of unacceptable behavior to take place and avoids "bailing out" the child.

Take Time-Out

Time-out is an effective tool in helping children gain self-control, especially in situations such as sibling fighting or temper fits. The Bible affirms this solitude by mentioning various times that our Lord retreated to be alone with himself and his Heavenly Father (see Matt. 14:23 and Luke 5:16).

Tony, the father of twin ten-year-old boys, uses time-out when the boys are losing control. "During time-out, the boys go to their rooms and spend time alone. There is no mandatory sentence writing or strict ritual such as putting their heads in the corner. Rather, they must stay in the rooms and calm down—away from parents and other stimulation such as television or video games. It not only helps the boys, but it also helps me gain self-control again."

We have found time-out to be helpful when our children need to get in control—when a child is about to lose control. During this period the child goes to his room and spends time alone. There is no punishment while in the room other than being alone. After a period of time, depending on the child's age and the type of behavior, the parent comes to retrieve the child with talk of improving the behavior.

Time-out is beneficial for many reasons. We have found that not only does the parent avoid overreacting to childish quarrels, but also the child benefits by being alone for a period with his inner thoughts. Often when a child has negative behavior, he has usually over-extended his coping resources for the day. Perhaps this is from playing too hard, not enough sleep, or too much stimulation. Whatever the reason, time-out gives the child an excuse to lie quietly on the bed, listen to a record, or read a good book.

In our large family, we frequently experience sibling quarrels. Sometimes it is impossible to tell who started the argument or fight. Time-out helps both parties get in control as they stay apart for a period of time.

Time-Out Works Best with a Positive Time-In

For maximum effectiveness, time-out must be an infrequently used part of a well-planned system of discipline that emphasizes and rewards good behavior while it punishes misbehavior. According to Stephen J. Bavolek, Ph.D., executive director of the Family Nurturing Center in Park City, Utah, time-out never works unless the "time-in" is positive.[6]

When the child is repentant and promises to have better behavior, look for something positive to compliment when the child interacts with family members or peers. Reinforcing good behavior is just as important as reflecting in time-out.

Time-Out Is Healthful for Parents

Time-out is also beneficial to tired, stressed-out parents, especially on days when the world seems to fall apart. This quiet time away from children allows you to get back in control. A quiet retreat to your room to be alone, outside to water and rewater the lawn, or even soaking in a warm bath can save you from unnecessary explosions that can ultimately hurt family members. Usually, after experiencing solitude for awhile, you can approach any situation at home with a fresher outlook as you collect inner thoughts and survey the situation with a calmer frame of mind.

Hold Family Meetings

In the family meeting, the parent is still authoritative, but rules can be made with input from all members and can be evaluated periodically. Each child has a chance to offer suggestions and complaints, and the parents, while still in control, have the opportunity to express feelings calmly. Understanding can occur as limits and consequences are set with the entire family consenting.

Family meetings can be held weekly with emergency meetings called when necessary. In our home, before our weekly meeting, each family member is encouraged to make a list of "complaints and challenges" to share. Before a negative complaint or challenge can be voiced, a positive compliment must lead. The complaint cannot be critical of any person.

Instead, the speaker must talk only of an act that occurred, a rule that was broken, or more freedom that is desired.

Compliment: "I like the way Ashley studied so hard this week without being reminded."
Challenge: "Ashley needs to spend some time cleaning out her room this week."

Compliment: "Brittnye, thank you for vacuuming the rugs without being told on Saturday. That was very responsible."
Challenge: "Brittnye, you need to watch turning your radio up too loud during the evening as it disturbs Ashley."

Compliment: "Rob, I like the way you taught me to play the guitar last weekend."
Challenge: "Could you please remember to close your door when you play the guitar late at night?"

Compliment: "Mom, thank you for fixing the hem on my skirt. "
Challenge: "Mom, when you get up early on Saturday morning, would you please try to be quieter? That is my only morning to sleep in."

Giving a compliment at the family meeting helps to build a receptive attitude for the behaviors that need changing. This also teaches the children that kindness can be shown as changes in behavior are suggested.

Establish House Rules at Family Meetings

House rules can be decided at family meetings, and while all parties might not agree to these, at least parents have an open forum in which to discuss their importance.

These are some of our house rules:

➤ Everyone is responsible for his or her room, including changing sheets, dusting, and vacuuming.

➤ Everyone is responsible for getting up on school days and Sundays and must be on time for rides to school or church.

➤ Going to church is not a choice; we will go as a family each week.

➤ Our home is a family affair, with everyone pitching in to get the chores done. If something needs cleaning or picking up, do it!

➤ Study hall is from 7:00 to 9:00 P.M. every school night.

➤ Only one half-hour of TV per day on school days unless there is a special program.

➤ If you talk back to an adult, you will lose TV, video games, or phone calls with friends for one day and night.

➤ If you do your chores, you will receive an allowance.

In the family meeting, rules can be evaluated periodically. Each child has a chance to offer suggestions, reasons, and complaints; the parent has the opportunity to express his feelings calmly. Understanding can occur as limits and restrictions are set with the entire family in agreement.

A family meeting is an important place for a parent to admit that he or she is wrong. Remember the saying, "Love means you never have to say that you are sorry?" Actually, real love frequently says, "I'm sorry." An apology to your children and spouse, along with God's forgiveness, is vital in building deep relationships and in recapturing the meaning of "family" in your home. You communicate respect to all members when you say, "I am wrong, and I'm sorry."

As you begin family meetings as a means of regaining control, be specific in outlining the expected behavior for your child. Remember, children are not born disciplined or understanding family rules, and they are not mind readers.

Write Out Behavior Contracts

Some families that are in control use behavior contracts with great success. "I write specific behavior contracts with my children every few weeks," Wanda, a single mother of two elementary-age girls, said. "I tell them what is expected, and we word this in a way they can understand. They add creative touches and sometimes color the contract. Each contract is signed, then if it is broken, the discussed consequences are administered."

If the girls break the contract, Wanda utilizes consequences such as not allowing television for several nights, no allowance for the week, no phone calls from friends, or no spend-the-nights on the weekend. "After working all day, I am too tired to continually ask the girls to help out, and I refuse to yell at them to get them to mind me. The contracts have solved the problem for us."

Be a Role Model

Being a positive role model—where the adult respects the child and vice versa—is most important in raising disciplined children. Howard, the father of five young children, said that parenting a large family challenges him to a Christian lifestyle that is beyond reproach.

"Because of my commitment to guide these children, I find my behavior, speech, and actions must lead the way—all week long," Howard shared. "The children see me as an example to follow. I guess my kids may consider me as the best Christian they know, so I am determined to take time to set the example in the home by respecting each child, dealing with daily discipline problems, and living a life according to Jesus' teachings."

Children watch everything we do; as Christian parents, we must also watch what we do!

The Teen Years:
Focus on What Is Really Important

As children approach teen years, they go from dependent children into independent young adulthood. While this transformation is not easy or pleasant, it is normal. You will get through the teen years—if you don't major on the minors. What does that mean? It means that as a parent you might lose some lesser battles, especially when the child you once carried to his room now towers over you and even has a very reasonable argument as to "why" he should or should not do what you said. All of a sudden, a simple "because it is in your best interest" may not seem appropriate. You think inside, "This child makes sense. My rules are too harsh. I'm over-reacting." But how does a parent back down without appearing weak or uncaring?

As the child hits teenage years, suddenly the family's rules begin to change. Whereas a parent may have emphasized tucking shirts in, cleaning the bedroom, and eating vegetables as being important in younger years, now it is more important to focus attention on responsible behavior outside the family, nightly curfews, morals and values, and respect for parents and teachers. In his book *Ten Mistakes Parents Make with Teenagers,* author Jay Kesler tells of some very important issues for parents of teens, including "respect for authority, including God, the government and parents; developing a giving, generous spirit; honesty; integrity; trustworthiness; stick-to-it-iveness." [7]

As teens begin to assert control at home, their bedrooms may become messy or even unapproachable. Their shirttails may never be tucked in, and they may openly tell you, "I will never eat broccoli again!" But the wise parent at this stage will weigh the teen's behavior with his new rebellion to see where to draw the line. If the teen is happy, respectful, makes good grades, can be trusted, and follows the important family rules, then a sloppy room once in a while is just that—his sloppy room. A closed door may be the best signal you can give while you affirm the positive behavior the teen has. A shirttail hanging out or vegetables left on the plate all of a sudden seem like a minor power struggle compared to parent-teen conversations about personal integrity or living a Christ-centered life or sexual abstinence until marriage. It is important to know when to change your parenting focus as your child asserts his new independence.

Do Not Let Go Too Soon!

"I'm so concerned about Shannon," a mother of an active sixteen year old told a group at our church the other night. "She has left the house with a different group every night this summer. I have no idea where they are going."

"I know what you mean," a single parent of two teens said. "Jason is always telling me he is at Sandy's house. Yet when I called Sandy's the other evening, no one was at home. Who knows where that kid is."

Why is it that when young people reach their midteen years, many parents give up the responsibility for raising them? Some concerned mothers and fathers admit defeat as their young person takes the family car and goes where he or she pleases. Many parents express fear that the young person may rebel if they make restrictions or limits too harsh.

At a counseling session, one parent told of allowing her young son to leave home at midnight to meet a group of boys. "He never knew that I was aware he was sneaking out," she admitted tearfully. "Yet I was so afraid if I stopped him, he would run away for good."

Many well-meaning parents express fear of their teenagers. As the child begins to tower over the parent in height and weight, a sense of authority is relinquished to him. Still, while the youth may appear mature physically, his emotions are still that of his age—quite young. Just because a six-foot tenth grader looks like a man is no reason to treat him as such. In fact, teenagers still need personal limits, restrictions, and the tremendous amount of care that they received as younger children.

One of the biggest temptations faced by the parent of a teenager is to let go too soon—to allow the youth to make his own decisions, set his own curfews, and determine his long- and short-term goals. When parents allow the teen too much freedom, the young person can make mistakes which are often damaging.

Perhaps the following suggestions can assist you in keeping a firm, loving hand on your teen.

Know Their Friends

Get to know your teen's friends. Invite them over to your home for snacks, or treat them to a fast food dinner at the local hangout. Become interested in their music, activities, and sports events. Watch for symptoms that may surface from a companion that may not be suitable for your child. As you receive proof that the companion is a negative influence, discuss your feelings and fears openly with your teen. Express your reasons for not wanting the child to associate with the friend and stand firm in your demands. Especially during the teen years, when peers become vital in feeling secure, your child needs guidance in choosing responsible friends.

Often the antics of the independent, undisciplined child appear exciting and entice the child from a more sheltered background. This gives even more reason for caring parents to intervene.

The teen years are the final chance to give your child a healthy start into responsible adulthood. By personally knowing his friends, being aware of what they are doing and where they hang out, the concerned parent can finish the quality parenting task they began at birth.

Continue to Set Firm Limits

"What do you mean I can't date until I am sixteen?" the physically mature teen complains. "You are so old-fashioned."

Setting limits for your teenager continues the caring that was felt in earlier years. Dating at sixteen, reasonable curfews at night, and specific evenings at home for just family members help teens to keep their age in perspective. The youth who begins dating at an early age often demands more sexual freedom at an early age.

If a junior high teenager is allowed to come in when he pleases, no wonder the high school youth feels free to stay out all night. Restricting dating and evenings out allows the family more time to influence the young person's development.

Just as a child needs limits for healthy development, the youth needs an authority figure in his life. The caring parent will allow their teenager a chance to become independent slowly and on firm ground—that is, with some limits and restrictions. The parent and child will experience interdependence as the young person returns home years later saying, "I'm glad you cared enough to say no."

Intervene When Necessary

"I think he is skipping school, but I'm not sure."

"Charles might be experimenting with drugs. He sleeps all day long."

Perhaps you have a faint hint that your child may not be staying inside his limits. If the child were seven years old, you would not hesitate in finding out what kind of mischief he was in and putting a stop to it. But, because a teenager looks mature, a parent often hesitates in seeking answers, and confronting the youth.

One of the best ways to really know what is going on in your teen's life is to keep communication open. Talk with him about his activities. Do not accuse, yet express your concerns.

Listen carefully and with empathy to his fears and questions. Is peer pressure a problem for your teen? How could you build his self-esteem so he could make responsible decisions?

Secure information that is firm and factual on drug, alcohol, and sexual abuse, and talk openly about the dangers and consequences of experimenting with these (see related information in chapter 4). If the child admits to having a problem, push away your pride and seek immediate professional help. Your pastor can guide you to the appropriate agency. Too many young people have wasted their lives because a parent had too much pride to admit defeat.

The teen years are still governed by the parent. Intervention and concern are just as necessary as ever in order to assure that the youth develops to maturity safely.

Encourage Christian Fellowship

"Should I make my child go to church or to youth activities?" Parents frequently ask this question of youth ministers and pastors. Most Christian educators feel that a teen should go to church, that the choice is not one they should make until full maturity. Yet these professionals also add that the family should go together to church as well. This means not dropping the youth off, but participating together in worship, fellowship, and group interaction.

If your teen rebels (and many do), become active with him. Volunteer to teach his Sunday School class, lead a Bible study, or drive a group of youth to a weekend retreat. Invite the young people from the church to your home for parties or rap sessions. Stay involved as long as it takes for your youth to keep an active place in the group.

Christian fellowship is vital for everyone. For the young person, this group offers answers to personal questions, allows for time to make decisions for Christ, and helps him to feel okay as other youth share experiences similar to his. A Christian lifestyle is learned in local church groups.

What About Spanking?

Twenty years ago, spanking was a more accepted method of discipline than it is today. Today spanking is shunned as a negative force in the family by most child experts. As we evaluate all the many methods of discipline from family meetings to time-out to logical consequences, spanking seems to rear an angry head because of its violent nature—many parents spank when they are totally out of control or angry. When an adult has lost control and strikes a child, there is always the fear, "Did I hit him too hard?" No parent should live with that fear!

Parents can be authoritative and firm disciplinarians in the home without striking a child, and this does not mean you are "sparing the rod." To "spare the rod" means not disciplining the child. Taking away worldly pleasures such as television, radio, video games, telephones, or playing with friends are probably more likely to get a child's attention and call for behavioral changes than hitting him. And when you use reasonable consequences, you never have to live with that horrible fear of physically hurting your child when you lose control. Stick to nonphysical methods of discipline, as they do work!

The Importance of Reflection

When our oldest son Rob was thirteen, he announced at dinner one night that he was now a "skater." Of course, we pretended not to know what this label meant and asked for a definition.

"Oh, that means that I am going to now have long bangs, wear baggy shorts and huge T-shirts, and carry my skateboard around with me all the time," he said with a thirteen-year-old's arrogance. I guess we looked a bit numb, for he added, "Didn't you do anything like this when you were thirteen?"

It was at that point that we learned a wonderful key to understanding children: reflect upon your own childhood or adolescent years before you make comments or judge the child.

"I think I was a 'surfer' when I was thirteen," Bob admitted that evening. "I remember wearing jams and baggy shirts and trying to bleach my hair blonde at the beach during the summer. I know my parents were humiliated, but a bunch of us hung out at the beach hoping to catch the mighty wave and become famous."

If it is difficult imaging Bob hanging ten on a slick board, think about Deb's own trendy behavior at thirteen.

"I remember everyone at that age letting their bangs grow long like the Beatles," Deb stated. "If you didn't have a 'Beatle-cut,' you could hardly face your peers. I developed this style of tossing my head so I could see through my long, thick bangs, and it drove my mother crazy."

Well, we lived with our "skater son" for twelve long months. Rob picked up the lingo, dressed the part, and learned to do fancy footwork on his four-wheeled board. He brought home "skater" friends and read "skater" magazines. Then just as suddenly as he became a "skater," he made a startling announcement at dinner while celebrating his fourteenth birthday.

"Parents," he announced boldly and with decisive maturity. "I've decided to throw away all my skating stuff and now as I prepare for high school, I'm going to be a 'prep.' I'll need some collared shirts and khaki pants, Mom, and may I get a haircut tomorrow?"

Again, we just listened as our son went through another stage in adolescence.

Rob became a prep that week, went on to high school, and became active in political action groups and student government. Now at age twenty, he continues to follow this conservative image and is a leader in his college community.

What did he teach us? We learned to reflect on our own teen years before commenting on strange apparel and behavior. We also have learned to ask "What would have helped us at that point in our teen life?" before making comments or criticism. This reflection has helped us to see that not all things children and teens say or do last forever. That is a blessing!

Everything Has Its Own Special Time

The writer of Ecclesiastes writes that everything has its own special time (see Eccles. 3:11). This is especially true with teens with their hormonal upswings who sometimes can be quite moody individuals.

Our middle daughter, Brittnye, was born into the world with a silver spoon in her mouth and since she began talking, has always wanted everything in her life to be "perfect." Well, being the very imperfect parents that we are, this has been a difficult goal for her. And as Brittnye entered her early teenage years, we began to see increasingly moody days and less positive ones.

"What are we doing wrong?" we asked her grandmother one morning at breakfast after our daughter sulked through her meal and left for the school bus without speaking. "We try to be friendly and upbeat, but she can only grumble that nothing suits her tastes."

"Maybe you should try leaving her alone in the morning," Grandmommy Jewel suggested wisely. "Perhaps you should allow her to make the first move in conversation and invite you both into her life."

Well, it was worth a try, for she was obviously reacting negatively to our morning friendliness. The next morning as we fixed breakfast for the other kids, we said nothing to her. We noticed that Brittnye looked up at us a few times to get our attention, but we quickly looked away.

Finally, she broke the ice. "Aren't you going to say 'good morning' to me, Mom and Dad?" she asked puzzled.

"Not anymore," we both agreed. "We've decided to let you start greeting us, but only if you want to."

She seemed a bit stunned at our answer and finished her breakfast. "Good breakfast, Mom. I love you, Dad," she said as she brought her plate to the kitchen. Then as she left for school, she called out, "Love you, too, Mom. I'll be home right after school."

We started our day that way for several months, with Brittnye leading the conversation and inviting us into her life. After awhile, when she seemed less moody, we asked her what the problem had been. She replied honestly, "Somehow, I got in a very bad mood when you both pushed me to be happy and friendly when I first woke up. When you quit talking to me, that made me sad, so I decided to start being friendly like you were. I felt better and didn't resent you then."

Who knows what was bothering her at the time. Call it teenage hormones or adolescent moodiness, but the important fact is that we were able to realize that, in time, she would be a loving daughter again. By addressing the problem, we learned how to stay in her life as we loved her each day.

Some Things Do Not Last Forever

Is it possible that our oldest children are both in college? Where did the time go? As we now watch our youngest daughter enter the ninth grade, we find it intriguing how she, too, has entered the world of the adolescent. We open her backpack and instead of finding completed papers, we see folded up notes written by her friends with such vital information as "Did you know who Tom likes now?" or "I forgot to bring my P.E. clothes. Can I borrow yours for fifth period?" The same notes that puzzled us with our first child are now understood as we realize peers are very important at this stage in her life.

We observe our middle daughter, now a freshman in college, and we are amazed at how she has matured. Is this sophisticated young woman the same moody preteen who resented parental authority? Now she begs for advice asking, "Mom, what would you do in this situation?" "Dad, don't forget to write me a love note this week." She disciplines her life telling friends, "I really can't go out tonight because I have a paper due." And she demonstrates compassion as she states matter-of-factly, "There is this girl in my dorm who looks so lonely, so I try to invite her to eat breakfast with me each morning."

What happened to that sloppy seventh grade boy who wore his shirts down to his knees and his sun-bleached bangs in his eyes? Where did he go? Is this the same young man who now is active in student government in college? Is this the same teen who calls home to "make sure the parents are well?" Is this the one who reads the Scriptures in church when a lay reader is needed?

Yes, childhood passes so quickly. This is not to say the experiences aren't painful at times, for most of us know that they are. But our teens have taught us that like anything in life, these years, too, shall pass. And if parents remain faithful to God through Christ's church as they nurture the teen, the end product of a mature, balanced Christian young person will usually be seen.

Keys to Positive Parenting

To review, the Bible describes many virtues in living the full Christian life. These virtues need to be discovered and used enthusiastically, especially when negative parenting moments tempt our patience. Perhaps the following suggestions can empower you become a positive parent even through trying moments in your life.

First, help your child develop trust in you as her parent. This trust lays the groundwork for her to later trust in God. Form the habit of praying often with your child. This helps her to know that God is a trusted friend and that He cares for her.

Second, firm discipline is vital for a child's self-esteem. Dr. Diana Baumrind of the University of California at Berkeley has studied how various types of parental control affect children. She has found that the most assertive, self-reliant, and self-controlled children had parents who were "controlling, demanding, communicative, and loving." In the same study, children with the least self-reliance had parents who were loving but noncontrolling and nondemanding.[8] While being loving and kind are important to boosting a child's self-image, equally important are firmness, rules, and regulations.

Third, let your child be free to be the special person God created. Labels are usually developed out of habit, by continually emphasizing only one dominant trait in a person. And while the label may sometimes be positive, the remark is usually derogatory.

One of the greatest hazards in labeling your child is that it limits the person's God-given potential. A teenager who is labeled as "wild" in your family may try to live up to his name. A meek child who is considered "introverted" may never break out of his shell.

Your ideas and perceptions of your children should change daily as situations allow. Often we keep a fixed opinion of what a person is like and then never allow for change or growth.

Encourage your children to realize their full potential as you help them build on their strengths. Give each child a chance to shine in a special way, whether it is in family responsibilities, personal talents, dealing with friends, or even preparing the family meal. Avoid comparing the children with each other. Instead, accept each child's uniqueness and realize that God made us to complement one another.

Fourth, let your child feel free to express emotions, concerns, personal joys, and frustrations without fear of being ridiculed. During times of family interaction and discussion, interject your own personal history. Tell of struggles you had as a child, a teen, and a young adult. Tell how God helped you cope with crises or disappointments. Mention how you felt in the situation—afraid, nervous, empty. Talk about your emotions in terms your children can understand—the pounding heart that accompanies being afraid or nervous; the pain in the stomach that goes with loneliness; the dull feeling that goes with mild depression.

Here are some basic discipline tips:

➤ When you say no, mean it. Do not argue with the child or let him wear you down with pleading and begging.
➤ Praise any good behavior. If the child is in a "negative rut," look for something positive to say.
➤ If you are wrong, admit it. Parents need to say "I'm sorry" or "I was wrong." This lets children see us as genuine.
➤ Have confidence. Establishing limits, rules, and consequences takes confidence on the parent's part. Know that what you are doing is best for the child.

Consistent Discipline Takes Sacrifice

An older friend of ours, Bill, and his wife were attending the college graduation of their two sons in a nearby city—one boy receiving his B.A. in Business and the other receiving his M.S. in Health Science. Both boys were outstanding young adults in their college community, having worked part time as they attended college, volunteered in the community with Little League baseball, and served as youth counselors at a local church. Both young men were also graduating Summa Cum

Laude from the college and received leadership honors from campus activities.

After the graduation ceremonies, a professor came over, and said, "I'll bet you are both so proud of those boys. You know, my wife and I would give anything to have raised decent and respectful kids like yours."

My friend said that he looked at his wife, then at his two boys, and spoke quietly, "We did." Twenty-two years of faithfully disciplining his boys flashed across his mind that moment, from attending church each week as a family to no television on school nights to attending school functions and parent-teacher conferences to long talks and administering consequences when the boys broke the rules. "Yes," our friend, Bill, told the professor. "We gave everything we had to raise our family."

Reclaiming the family with loving and consistent discipline is not something that can happen overnight. Raising good kids in a Christian home means you will spend a great deal of time and energy. It means setting limits and establishing and enforcing consequences—even when you are tired or busy or distracted. And so often it entails "giving anything and everything" to have responsible children as our friend said.

There are many effective ways to discipline children in a Christ-centered home, including methods not described in this chapter. But we have chosen to tell you what we have used and what has worked in our home. Just as children change from day to day, we have had to rely on different methods, varying these as we tried to catch the attention of our three. But the most important factor to remember as you become a disciplined family is that parents have to be authoritative—following through day-in and day-out as the experts, giving limits and consequences to their young.

Does a positive, Christian atmosphere permeate your home? A family that is secured in God's love through Jesus

Christ will be eternal—"A cord of three strands is not quickly torn apart" (Eccl. 4:12). Reclaiming the family with strong discipline is not an easy task. As you set parenting goals for your family with God leading the way, you can begin to experience this ultimate sense of hope, purpose, and great expectation.

Family Time

Doing Some "Home" Work

➤ Have a family meeting with all members. Have each family member make a list of "complaints and compliments" as discussed on page 77. Remind them that before a negative complaint can be aired, a positive compliment must be shared. With the complaint, focus only on the act, not the person involved. Make a list of their "complaints and compliments" and post this on the refrigerator for the upcoming week.

➤ During your family meeting, make time to establish "home rules." let all members participate and offer their opinion as to what is fair and what is not. Be sure these rules refer to bedtimes, chores and responsibilities, curfews for teens, dress code, television habits, homework times, phone rules, and more. Write these rules on a sheet of paper, have each family member sign this, then post on the refrigerator.

➤ Have members decide on appropriate consequences (with parental guidance) if a rule should be broken. Make a list of these consequences such as losing a toy, no television for the night, time out for a certain period of time, or missing a party or outing on the weekend. have all members sign this sheet and post it next to the list of family rules.

Notes

1. "Dr. Spock had it right," *U.S. News & World Report*, August 7, 1989, 49.

2. Jay Kesler, *Ten Mistakes Parents Make with Teenagers*, (Brentwood: Wolgemuth & Hyatt, Publishers, Inc., 1988), 58.

3. "Dr. Spock had it right."

4. "Discipline Made Easier" by Ron Taffel, *McCall's*, February 1992, 98.

5. "Dr. Spock had it right," 50.

6. "Making Time-Out Work" by Dena K. Salmon, *Parent's*, February 1992, 98.

7. Kesler, *Ten Mistakes*, 71.

8. Jeane Westin, *The Coming Parent Revolution* (Chicago: Rand, McNally, & Company, 1981), 188–89.

Chapter 3

Take Control Through Communication

Communication is vital for families in control. When communication breaks down, the family breaks down. In fact, when communication breaks down, everything breaks down. Take the Walters family, for example. "We just can't talk." That's how Thomas describes his relationship with his two teenage daughters. When the three sit down to talk about school, church events, or even their favorite ball team, the conversation is strained. Thomas does not know what to say to the girls and always wishes the moment was over. "I know I seem nervous when we try to communicate, but I work long hours at the shop, and I hardly ever see my daughters."

But communication is necessary in order for families to thrive. Communication is so important that a popular magazine polled over thirty thousand women and only one problem ranked above conflicts over money—poor communication. Studies show that if they had it to do again, many women say they would pick a husband who had the ability to communicate.

Communication gaps in families—even in Christian families—are a fact of life. But there are ways to encourage communication as you become genuine and approachable in your parent-child relationship.

Let us start with some communication basics.

Are You a Good Communicator?

Some of us are definitely more talented than others at communicating. Our friend Carmel has such a gift. Whenever she is at a school or community meeting, there is always a circle of people around her, sharing problems and concerns. And you can tell that her attention is fully on the person speaking. Carmel stands attentive and looks the person she is talking with straight in the eye, never allowing herself to be distracted by others in the room. Yes, she has the gift of communicating.

But what about in the family? What does it take for a parent to communicate with the other members? Here are some criteria that are important.

➤ The parent is approachable: Your child can talk to you without hesitation or fear.

➤ The parent shows genuine concern: You are not too busy or preoccupied but are attentive with family members.

➤ The parent is open-minded: You express yourself with your child and speak in a manner they can understand.

➤ The parent exhibits concern by their mannerism and tone of voice: All the family members are important to you.

➤ The parent acts like an adult: You act your age, not like an older teenager.

➤ The parent represents control: You are in control of the family and do not have to lose your temper or yell to receive attention.

Do you fit the criteria of a good communicator? As much as we would like, not many of us can have all these qualities every day. In our home, one of us might seem more attentive than the other at night, depending on how tiring our day was. But we all can and must work on our communication skills. We must make special efforts to erase stumbling blocks from the past and move on to greater understanding and love.

Throw Away Your Schedule Book

How can you communicate with someone if you never spend time with them? Many parents who have lost control of the family are so concerned about financial gain or career mobility that time alone with the children is nil. "Time with the kids? I can't fit that into my schedule this week," a father of two teenage boys said.

Journalist Ellen Goodman of the *Boston Globe* tells a heartwarming story of how Senator Paul Tsongas regards family time as a top priority.

> I met Paul Tsongas once on a late-afternoon flight from Washington to Boston. The senator from Massachusetts was traveling light that day. No bags, no briefcase, no aides. All he had with him was a daughter.
>
> It was rare enough to see a man alone on a plane with a preschool child. But Tsongas's reason reason was even more unusual. He was going to Boston for a meeting, and he wanted to spend more time with his middle daughter. So he was taking her along for the ride. Together they would get the late plane back.
>
> I've thought about that scene a dozen times, with mixed feelings of admiration and poignancy. Here was a father who had to capture minutes with his child, on the fly, at 35,000 feet.

This scene, repeated over and over again in Tsongas's life, seems somehow symbolic of a whole generation of men and women: parents with schedule books. It is barely even a parody of the way many of us cram work and children into calendars that won't expand to fill the needs, into lives that cry out for more hours. Tsongas was one of us, trying to make it all fit together.

But last October, the senator and father of three young girls discovered something that wasn't on his agenda. He had a tumor that was "not benign." . . . The statistical average life expectancy for those with this disease (mild lymphoma), as he related it, is eight years, and he is planning for more. . . . But Tsongas decided not to run again. He is coming home to Lowell, Mass., and home to his family in a way that politics doesn't allow.

. . . Tsongas never forgot the older colleague who stopped by his table when he was a freshman congressman and said, "Let me tell you one thing. I was in your shoes. I was here and I really devoted myself to my job and I ignored my kids and they grew up and I never knew them. It makes me very sad. Whatever you do, don't do that."

[Tsongas] had to hear the words "not benign" to finally focus on priorities, on mortality, on time itself. . . . There are times when we all end up completing a day or a week or a month, as if it were a task to be crossed off the list with a sign. In the effort to make it all work, it becomes all work. We become one-minute managers, mothers, husbands. We end up spending our time on the fly. [1]

A single pastor-friend of ours made a date with his two teenage sons every week for a dinner out, a walk on the beach, or a campout. "When my wife Helen died when the boys were young, I realized that I would have to communicate in a way that was firm and caring. So I make a special time with the boys each week, and nothing short of a crisis will make me break this," Bill said. "While we are together away from the television set and telephone, I tell them how much I love them and believe in them. We talk about problems we have and pray together for our family. At first they giggled and were embarrassed because it was so personal, but I've been doing this for eleven years now, and we all look forward to this special family time. No one can take away the bond we feel for one another." There is a father whose priorities are in their proper order! Yes, he makes time weekly, year after year, to be alone with his sons. Instead of periodically fitting his sons into his schedule book, this regular time apart from work to be intimate with his children has become a way of life.

Be an Effective Listener

In the book *Bus 9 to Paradise,* Leo Buscaglia tells about boarding a flight to New York. The flight attendant shouted with delight when he entered the plane. "I've wanted to meet you for such a long time. May I talk with you later?" she asked. When she got a break, the young woman sat next to him and frantically told her story—a cheating husband, a disturbed child, a feeling of despondency and helplessness, a fear of being unable to cope. After a long while, she stopped in mid-sentence and sighed deeply with relief. She wiped her tears and sat up in the seat. "Oh, Dr. Buscaglia," she said, "you've helped me so much." [2] Do we need to tell you that Dr. Buscaglia had not even uttered a word? What a tremendous ministry it is just to listen. Harmony at home begins with good communication, and this all starts with listening skills.

Being an effective listener in the family is vital in establishing a caring rapport. When feelings and thoughts are poured out in the family and real listening occurs, the speaker feels loved and understood.

"A good listener is nonjudgmental, accepts what the speaker is saying and lets it in," says Linda Goldea Klau, Ph.D., a psychologist from New York City. "Listening doesn't mean preparing for your half of the 'argument.' There is no right or wrong to any issue, only perspective and points of view. And we need to learn to experience different points of view rather than rejecting them. We need to be more committed to communication and understanding than to our own opinions."[3]

But communication in the family is different. It is amazing how well we listen to a good friend when we are interested in the subject. Yet what happens when the discussion is between parent and child? Often we tune out the conversation, ignore the child speaking, and use all sorts of body language to let him or her feel that we are not interested in his or her thoughts or opinion nor do we try to listen nonjudgmentally.

"Everytime we sit down to talk about school or dating, it turns into a big fight," Crystal, the mother of a seventeen-year-old girl, said. "I try to hear what she is telling me, but she is always wrong."

Often we do feel that our children are wrong, whether in their ideas or values or goals. But letting them know immediately that they are wrong only closes the door to further communication. And this further communication between a parent and child could enable the young person to make sense of his ideas and come to decisions that are well-thought-out and moral.

Let us analyze two families' listening skills. Which one conveys a message of caring and concern? Which describes your family?

I Hear What You Are Saying, But . . .

Mrs. White: "I see you still have not picked up the leaves in the yard, Jason."

Jason: "Well, I started picking them up, then I saw Mr. Smith coming home next door with his groceries, so I went over to help him bring the packages in. He seemed to be having a hard time lifting the bags."

Mrs. White: "That doesn't solve our problem, Jason. You still have not picked up the leaves."

Jason: "I will, Mom. But when I got back to my rake and the pile of leaves, it was dinnertime so I went in to eat."

Mrs. White: "I realize that, Jason. But you know my rules, and you still have not picked up the leaves."

Jason: "Well, I went out to finish the job after dinner then I remembered that I had band practice at 7:00 at school. I did three bags of leaves, Mom, and I will finish the rest after school tomorrow. But I really need to go now because we are learning the routine for Friday night's game. Couldn't I finish the leaves tomorrow?"

Mrs. White: "Jason, you know in this house rules are rules . . . and you still haven't picked up the leaves."

I Don't Agree, But I Understand

Mr. Caldwell: "Melissa, you promised your mother that your room would be cleaned by this afternoon before our company arrives."

Melissa: "I straightened most of it, Dad, but I have a mega report due tomorrow in Chemistry and I need to finish it."

Mr. Caldwell: "What kind of report is it?"

Melissa: "Actually it is a comparison between the different molecular combinations and the reactions they give off. It is my hardest subject, Dad, but I think I can pull a B in the course if I do a good job."

Mr. Caldwell: "Well, I want you to do your best. Chemistry was always my hardest subject, and I know the time it takes to figure out all of those combinations. But what about your room?"

Melissa: "I can make it presentable tonight, then really vacuum and dust it tomorrow. Okay?"

Mr. Caldwell: "Cleaning your room is your job at home, Melissa, but the report comes first. Go ahead and complete the report, then tomorrow after school focus on your room."

How Do You Rate?

Which parent are you? Do you really listen to the needs your child expresses and weigh each situation with compassion and empathy? Or do you make rules that are never to be broken and ignore the reasons your child suggests?

As Christian parents we have the perfect example of Jesus Christ to follow in our lives. He patiently listened to each person who approached Him, empathized with their problems, and shared that selfless love with others while communicating.

Healthy families use signs, symbols, body language, smiles and other gestures to express caring and love. They deal with silence and withdrawal in a positive, open way. Communication does not mean just talking or listening; it includes all the clues to a person's feelings—his bearing, her expression, their resignation. Family members do not have to say, "I'm hurting," or "I'm in need." A quick glance tells that. And they have developed ways of responding that indicate caring and love, whether or not there is an immediate solution to the pain.[4]

Parents who are good listeners can hear the nonverbal clues that there might be a problem with their child:

> Slammed doors
> Unusual silence in the bedroom
> Locked doors for long periods of time
> Behavior that regresses—temper fits, crying jags, hitting other siblings
> Sullen looks
> Restlessness
> Insomnia

➤ Lack of appetite; overeating
➤ Irritability

As you work toward greater communication in the family, try to become a more effective listener by letting your children know that they are accepted—unconditionally. As you make a conscious effort to listen and to understand each individual, your child will begin to express his or her innermost thoughts to you; a relationship is formed.

Communication Skills

Parenting expert John Rosemond gives the "Three C's of Good Communication" in the book *John Rosemond's Six-Point Plan for Raising Happy, Healthy Children.* They include the recommendation to:

1. Be Commanding.
2. Be Concise.
3. Be Concrete.

Parents can sum up these points by standing firm as they talk with their children, always stating the problem in a manner that is authoritative, using as few words as possible to get the message across, and speaking in language that is easily understood and not vague. Firm communication should be directive but fair, as the parent seeks the best for the child and expects him to obey.

Practice Give-and-Take

Healthy family communication involves give-and-take by the members. Your child might say, "I think this is right." You retort, "But I feel it is wrong." And another member pitches in, "Well, I disagree with both of you." And all of this is done in the spirit of love and acceptance. How can that be?

Give-and-take offers family members practice in speaking their minds, offering their viewpoint, and learning to stand up for what they believe to be true. Some families call this type of communication argumentative; in our home we call it typical and exhausting! But the family is a safe testing ground where children learn what is acceptable language, behavior, and values and what is not. Only by asserting their opinions in family conversations can children truly test their personal beliefs. Parents need to recognize this as a testing ground and allow children to state their viewpoints during family conversations. Of course, this does not mean that your children can follow through on opinions they might share. That is where limits are set with parents deciding what is right and wrong for the child.

Encourage Your Child to Express Feelings

A family that has healthy communication allows the members to ventilate and express their innermost feelings. Children should feel that they can express emotions, concerns, personal joys, and frustrations in appropriate ways without fear of being ridiculed. We have found that such a secure atmosphere where feelings can be expressed can only happen if we lead the way.

During times of family discussion, we try to interject our personal history, telling of struggles we had as teenagers and young adults. We share how God helped us cope with crises or disappointments and mention how we felt in the situation— afraid, nervous, empty. Talking about our emotions in terms our children can understand is especially helpful in being genuine—the pounding heart that accompanies being afraid or nervous; the pain in the stomach that goes with loneliness; the dull feeling that goes with sadness. We allow our children the privilege of knowing that "Mom and Dad have been there too." Knowing that a "normal" adult has experienced these feelings soothes the child as they accept their feelings and express them appropriately.

As we have risked being open and have talked about our life struggles as Christians, our children have learned to trust us and feel comfortable enough to express their feelings within the safety of our family.

Communicate Compassion in the Family

Compassion is the ability to feel with another person. We need to take a second look at our spouses and our children and ask ourselves, "Do I have any understanding of the experiences that have brought him or her to this place in life? Is there anything I can do to make his life or her life easier and more meaningful?"

What a wonderful asset a sense of compassion is in the family! There is a story about two brothers who were spending their last days together in a nursing home. The brother in the bed closest to the window was warm, talkative, outgoing, optimistic, and altogether very sociable. The brother next to the door was blind, negative, and quite lonely.

One day the brother next to the door asked the brother next to the window to describe for him the things that were going on outside. The brother next to the window took great delight in doing so. He described colorful flowers bursting into bloom and delicate hummingbirds feeding from the buds; he told how the mothers were pushing babies in strollers and children were laughing on the playground. This became a daily ritual as the jovial brother next to the window described to his blind brother the flurry of activity outside. The brother who was blind lived for these reports from outside.

But one day the sensitive, extroverted brother next to the window died, and his bed was taken by another man. "Would you please describe for me," asked the surviving brother next to the door, "what is going on outside our window?" The new roommate looked out the window in puzzlement and then looked back at the man, saying, "I don't see what good it would do, my friend. There is nothing outside this window except a dirty brick wall."

This story illustrates how God calls families to "feel with" one another. God gives us compassion. How about in your family? Does someone have a stumbling block that you can help with? Is there a member experiencing conflict to whom you can offer empathy? Can you help someone who may be bitter from past failures see God's plan for their life?

In Paul's letter to the Ephesians, he writes, "And His gifts were varied; He Himself appointed and gave men to us, some to be apostles (special messengers), some prophets (inspired preachers and expounders), some evangelists (preachers of the Gospel, traveling missionaries), some pastors (shepherds of His flock) and teachers. His intention was the perfecting and the full equipping of the saints (His consecrated people), that they should do the work of ministering toward building up Christ's body (the church)" (Eph. 4:11–12, AMP).

The amazing affirmation Paul makes here is that these differences are given to us to help us build each other up to maturity and to grow up in love. When we push and tug against each other in the family we begin to discover who we are; we begin to grow into the persons God intended. When we compassionately reach out to family members "even, though . . . " God will bless our homes.

Healthy growth and communication in the family involves a kind of transformation—the movement from that place where we wish everyone were like us to the place where we are so accustomed to their idiosyncrasies and their special quirks that we wonder how we ever got along without them. A family is the place where people are able to accept each other and like each other in the midst of their problems, fears, and shortcomings. Although that sounds difficult, under the control of the love of God in a Christ-centered home, all the unique parts of the body work together so that the body can build itself up and grow in love.

Is there room for compassion in your family today? Have you transformed your family to where everyone is accepted—even though they may be different? Let God unite your family through compassionate communication as you recapture the meaning of unity at home.

Speak the Truth in Love

Paul also urges us to "speak the truth in love" (Eph. 4:15). This means that in the family we must work to speak plainly and clearly with one another. Sometimes we have to say, "I am angry" or "I am hurt" or "I am disappointed." When we can trust our own feelings and face the truth of who we are, then we can move forward as a unit.

There is danger at the other end of the spectrum. Just as some cannot speak the truth to those they love, others use the truth as a club to beat their family into submission and to blackmail the members to get what they want.

Paul does not tell us to simply "speak the truth." He admonishes that we are to "speak the truth in love" saying, "Do not let any unwholesome talk come out of your mouth, but only what's helpful for building others up according to their needs, that it may benefit those who listen. Get rid of all bitterness, rage and anger, brawling and slander, along with every form of malice. Be kind and compassionate to one another, forgiving each other, just as in Christ God forgave you" (Eph. 4:29–32).

Learn to Forgive

One of the worst lies ever perpetrated on the American public came from the movie *Love Story.* Do you remember the phrase that was plastered across billboards, newspaper advertisements and handbills—"Love means never having to say you are sorry"?

As you reclaim your family and bring together years of accumulated memories—some bitter and angry—lean on the forgiveness that Jesus Christ taught. As you grow together in your family relationship and begin to communicate in love, allow forgiveness to enter into your hearts. Knowing that you are forgiven by God in Christ empowers you to love and forgive others. Jesus said, "If you do not forgive others, your Heavenly Father cannot forgive you." In our families, we cannot claim forgiveness from God until we begin to experience forgiveness from others and until we forgive those around us (see Bob's personal testimony of forgiveness in the introduction).

Relax! You Do Not Have to Know All the Answers

"Ask Mom. She'll know." Or, "Dad always knows the answer. Ask him." These are common statements in our home as questions fly nightly regarding homework, peer relationships, what outfit to wear, and more. And at times we have felt as if we had to know all the answers—spiritually and emotionally. In fact, sometimes it has been quite embarrassing not to have a correct response to a child's question. However, admitting that we don't know is the first way of letting the three Bruce children know that we are real and approachable.

Linda, the parent of four teenagers, commented: "The entire time I was growing up, I always thought my parents knew everything about life. When I was in seventh grade, my dad became angry at me for asking so many questions about my faith. Then he admitted that he didn't know the answers either. It wasn't until I became a parent of teenagers that I began to feel this pressure of being 'on stage.' I wouldn't have respected my dad any less for being honest and admitting that he didn't know the answers to questions. I am determined to be upfront with my children and admit my frailty as a human, then point them in the best direction for answers."

We have learned that the best way to help children find answers to their questions is to direct them to proper resources—the Bible, an encyclopedia, a peer, our pastor, a teacher, their doctor, the youth director at church, or a specialist in the questioned field. A parent must lead as the shepherd, but the world is full of knowledgeable and experienced resources that can help young people to find answers.

Communicate Through Touch

The significance of touch in human development was first identified in the 1940s. Many institutionalized infants, who were either homeless or had been orphaned because of the war, suffered from what doctors then called marasmus, which literally means wasting away; this is now known as a failure to thrive. Well-fed but unloved, some babies even died. Those who survived showed impaired physical and mental development.

However, doctors discovered that just a few minutes a day of talking, maintaining eye contact, and stroking helped these hospitalized babies grow and mature at the same rate as home-reared babies. The reason these babies could not thrive seemed to lie in the message a lack of contact conveyed, a message that said, "No one is here to care for you."[5]

Touch is critical in becoming genuine and real with our children. We have found that by offering those extra strokes and hugs especially when our three teens are not so lovable, caring is felt. A pat on the shoulder, a hug, a firm handshake, or other strokes often generate a stronger sense of caring and concern than spoken words.

In his ministry, Jesus expressed concern and healed many persons with his hands. In the story of Jesus receiving the little children despite his disciples' objections, "He took the children up in his arms, put his hands on them and blessed them," (Mark 10:16, NIV). When Peter's mother-in-law was ill, Jesus "touched her hand and the fever left her" (Matt. 8:15, NIV).

Can you visualize our Lord lifting his arms around children, lifting up the lame, and embracing those in pain? As He preached love and concern, He also demonstrated them. He reached out with gentle, caring hands, touching cold and empty lives with His power.

Your children may be hiding behind masks or feeling insecure about their place in family or peer group, and a loving touch may be the security they need.

Here are some touch tips you can use with your family. First, try hugging your child after you have reprimanded him. Somehow, all the anger you felt toward the child is eased as you hold him close and express your love with a gentle hug.

Second, some children, especially boys, seem to "run" from hugs, when learning to give and receive this type of affection can enable them to recognize their true feelings as they mature. Find times during the day to give your child a big "bear" hug. Lift him off his feet! Let him know that it is okay to hug someone he cares about.

Third, teach your child the rules about "good touch—bad touch." Let them know that no one should ever touch them in private places. A good rule of thumb is that no one should touch them on the part of the body that their bathing suit covers. Especially if your child is away from you and in the care of other adults, this point needs to be addressed frequently. Let your child feel comfortable to come to you and talk if he is ever concerned about this subject.

Can you get in twelve hugs each day? Try the following:

1. When the child wakes up—Good-morning hug.
2. After breakfast—I-love-you hug.
3. Before school—Have-a-good-day hug.
4. After school—I-missed-you hug.
5-8. Anytime—big-and-bountiful-bear hugs.
9. Before dinner—Wash-your-hands hug.
10. After dinner—I'm-glad-you're-mine hug.
11. After homework—I'm-proud-of-you hug.
12. Bedtime—Sleep-tight hug.

Enjoy One Another

After a full week of no television and study hall every night in preparation for final exams, our son said, "The only thing different about being a teenager is that before I got in high school, I used to laugh and have fun."

That free easy spirit of childhood does seem to diminish as we take on the responsibilities of young adulthood. But remember the fun times you used to have as a child? Perhaps it was bowling on Saturday morning or fishing late at night or picnics to the beach to watch the sunset. Making time to have fun with your children enhances the family relationship. Your fun times might be free and spur of the moment—like an early breakfast at a nearby restaurant before school or watching the late movie together on Saturday night. No matter how you play these light moments, they are vital in breaking down the barriers that occur between generations.

Communication Takes Time and Energy

Communication in the family does not just happen. While some of us are more talented at communicating than others, learning to speak to family members in a manner that conveys love and acceptance is a lifelong process. Open communication is one important attribute that you can establish in your parent-child relationship. The concerned, parent can set the firm foundation in building communication skill. You can help to bridge these gaps as you use techniques of effective communication, generate acceptance among members, and create an atmosphere of caring each day.

When There Is No One to Communicate With

A single mother spoke openly in the group about a struggle she was having. "I have the most difficult time getting my ten-year-old to come to Sunday School."

Another single parent, raising his two sons alone, said, "I am so uncertain of the biblical guidelines that I need to know for raising my children."

Raising children without the support of another adult is so difficult. Studies show that over 50 percent of all families are single parent homes. If parents cannot communicate with other adults in the home, the church can be responsible for offering groups of support and compassion. In these groups the biblical guidelines for parenting can be taught and interpreted so parents—married and single—have a firm foundation on which to build.

If you are a single parent—or married and not receiving the emotional support you need to reclaim the family—perhaps you need to communicate with other Christians about concerns that are hindering your family's growth. A parent support group can be an excellent support system for all parents within the local church. This group is composed of parents who meet together regularly to share problems, receive support, and find answers. These parents also receive biblical strength as the pastor or other group leader shares Scriptures that offer guidelines for Christian living.

This unique ministry not only provides a means for problems to be answered and for faith to be nurtured, it also enables church members to reach out to the community and relate a living Lord to the real concerns of the world.

The parent support group can meet at anytime, but it has greater participation when held in conjunction with a children's choir, craft group, or other children's activity. This way, the whole family will have a sense of unity as they come to the church together, and childcare is provided.

Although the pastor or other mature Christian should be in charge of the Scripture training, anyone can lead the sharing and discussion. Speakers and film series can be used effectively to give parents insight into the various problems that come with childhood stages. Pediatricians, child guidance counselors, and other professionals can be tremendous assets in explaining the stages of child development, behavioral problems, and methods of discipline.

Ideally, the parent support group should serve as a sounding board, allowing parents a safe place to ventilate their concerns, without fear of being criticized for their own methods of child rearing. This involves creating an atmosphere of love, caring, and understanding in which people are not afraid to speak.

Communication is this unique group's key to relieving tensions and fears. In one church, a single mother received comfort as she was referred to a counseling service to assist her young son. Another parent, after listening to a school counselor at the support group, was able to recognize early signs of a learning disability and sought professional help for his child. And all parents received assurance as they gained a better understanding of what God expected of them as they tackled the task of Christian parenting.

Specific topics that we found timely with a parent support group include: dealing with death, preparing for school, when both parents work, sibling rivalry, becoming responsible at home, handling schoolwork, and coping with divorce in families. Parents also find strength from answers to questions such as "Should I make my child attend church?" or "How can we study the Bible as a family?"

With the parent support group, Christian faith is strengthened as the family attends church together. As both parents and children engage in fellowship, sharing, and study, the church can extend its ministry to include parents while teaching God's message.

Do Not Let Anger Control Communication

Anger is expressed in every family. As your children get older, it is only normal for them to ventilate angry feelings when you hold firm to family rules. For some very strong-willed children, angry thoughts will be expressed when a parent firmly tells them "no." Temper fits, shouts of "I hate you," and aggressive acts such as kicking furniture are *not* abnormal. Most children experience feelings of anger or frustration at parents as they seek to lead independent lives.

Many factors can add to these real feelings of anger. Different situations in the home can affect the child and create violent feelings of rage and fury inside. Family members can irritate the child. Parent's rules and regulations can make the child feel too restricted. Responsibilities such as chores at home and homework can create anxiety in the child. But parents must teach coping tools to deal with anger.

When fourteen-year-old Lisa found out that her mother had to work late at the hospital on Friday, she knew she would have to miss the middle school football game to baby-sit her younger brother.

"My mom makes me so angry!" Lisa snapped to her friend Paul on the phone. "I never have known someone who was so selfish. I always have to give up my plans for the family, and if I don't, Mom puts me on a complete guilt trip."

After Lisa finished talking with Paul, she ran up the stairs and slammed the bedroom door in anger causing the antique mirror in the hallway to crash to the hard, wooden floor. One moment of uncontrolled anger created a devastating loss of several hundred dollars and years of family memories.

Carl became enraged at his father when he had to help paint the house instead of being allowed to go to the beach on Saturday with his friends. Filled with anger, Carl almost lost control of the car on the way to the hardware store.

"I was so angry at Dad that I pushed the accelerator instead of the brake," he said. "I lost control of the car, ran up on a curb, and almost hit a little boy on a bicycle."

Nine-year-old Chandra piercingly stared at her mother and let the painful words sink in. "If you don't stop talking back to me and start doing what I ask you, you will have no friends over this weekend," Mrs. Dearing had told her one morning before her big slumber party.

And all Chandra said was, "Yes, ma'am." Yet she wondered why her stomach ached all afternoon.

Like Lisa, Carl, and Chandra, all children experience conflict. These feelings of frustration and tension are quite normal as they seek independence. Our children only learn about themselves as they challenge the world around them. Testing and questioning the ideas of others are one of the primary ways they develop their own ideas—and their own identity. But this testing can often lead to conflict with parents. And conflict can lead to uncontrolled anger . . . if we allow it.

Eleven-year-old Tim said, "When I become frustrated or angry with anyone, I usually keep these real feelings inside instead of talking about the problem. But on days when I get really angry, I can't eat or sleep."

Some children learn to use anger in a positive manner, some ignore their anger, and others let their anger consume their whole being. As you administer discipline, you can also encourage your child to understand these angry feelings and replace the energy he or she spends in being angry with positive actions that will make life more pleasurable.

Understanding Anger

There are three types of anger: upfront, displaced, and inward. Understanding each type will help you know how to teach your child appropriate ways to handle it.

➤ Upfront anger is expressed directly toward the person or situation at which you are angry. This type of anger, if not overemphasized, is most acceptable as your child expresses feelings to the person involved. Statements such as "Yes, this rule makes me mad" or "I get so angry when you restrict me from television" are acceptable *if* your child does not follow through with violent outbursts.

➤ Displaced anger originates from strong feelings toward a person or event, but this is directed toward another person or event. For example, a parent may give the child only part of his allowance one week and suggest that "you help out the family more next week." Knowing that he did help out some, the idea that he may not have helped enough, can make your child furious. But instead of expressing this anger to you and explaining his side of the situation, your child screams or hits his younger sister, expressing displaced anger. This is the most painful anger as the child loses control and lets the steam blow by spewing harsh words on innocent victims.

➤ Inward anger is unexpressed, either verbally or nonverbally. Instead of speaking openly about his angry thoughts, the child lets it boil up inside and eat away at his entire being. For children who internalize their anger, the result can be physical ailments such as nausea, tension headaches, or muscle aches. Some children express anger as sarcasm toward others or even with criticism.

You can relax and know that it is very normal for your child to get angry, especially if firm discipline in the home is just now being introduced after years of permissiveness. But this does not give your child the right to devastate himself and others while expressing this anger in inappropriate ways. By holding onto angry feelings, he prevents himself from moving forward to a more positive outlook in life. And by verbally or physically lashing out at others, your child can hamper the relationships that are important in life.

The Bible has much to teach us about anger and about self-control. Share with your child how Jesus became angry in the synagogue. The marketing of wares in God's house on the Sabbath was certainly against principles He held close to His heart. Paul spoke of self-control during times of anger saying, "But when the Holy Spirit controls our lives, he will produce this kind of fruit in us: love, joy, peace, patience, kindness, goodness, faithfulness, gentleness, and self-control" (Gal. 5:22–23, TLB).

Helping your child develop self-control involves understanding his feelings and helping him deal with aggression constructively. Sometimes this is easier said than done!

Help Your Child Gain Self-Control

First, teach your child the hurt, frustration, or disagreement that is causing the angry feelings. Is the anger because of parent conflicts? Is your child mad because of not enough freedom or a curfew that is too early? Perhaps the anger stems from something your child did or said at home—lashing out at parents with backtalk or a fight with his brother or sister over who is to mow the lawn. Whatever is causing the problem, get your child to pinpoint exactly what is wrong, and try to deal with the feeling or emotion instead of the people involved.

Second, help the child to accept the feeling as being very real: "I am mad, and this is the way I feel." Accepting the hostility can help your child begin to find ways to reduce the tension by directing his feelings in appropriate ways that don't hurt people.

Third, teach the child to channel the angry feelings. Lashing out at parents or siblings only hurts those your child cares about. Angry words are very empty words after they are said, but these words can leave painful memories that last forever. Get your child to find a creative outlet for the angry feelings like riding a bike, jogging, cooking, or taking a time-out in his room while he gains self-control.

Fourth, remind the child to remove himself from the scene of frustration or hurt. Your child needs to learn to anticipate. Let him know that if you are tired after working all day, he may choose to wait until you have relaxed before approaching you with a problem that may cause conflict. If his brother his brother seems distant, give him space instead of being argumentative. If parents seem moody, do not choose that time to confront them. Your child can learn to be sensitive to these needs of others and find the appropriate time to talk about conflicts he may have.

Communication is the key in resolving angry feelings, but your child must also find the best moment to do this. Being direct and honest about the problem without being disrespectful is the best way to smooth harsh feelings.

The goal of learning to deal with anger in an acceptable manner is to move from anger to reconciliation. As your child accepts all of his feelings as being very real, remains sensitive to the views of others, and channels his anger in creative and appropriate ways, he can grow from childlike dependency to adult autonomy without many painful memories. And your home environment will run much smoother as you teach coping tools to dealing with this very normal emotion.

Anger Escapes for Parent and Child

➤ Prayer—Praying to God and feeling His power can help lessen the intensity of the anger. Ask Him to take away these feelings and replace them with His love.

➤ Exercise—Run, walk, ride bike, jump rope, play basketball, swim, dance.

➤ Music—Play the piano, drums, keyboard, flute or sing or listen to favorite tapes or CDs.

➤ Read—Read Scriptures that soothe you, study, read a favorite book.

➤ Cook—Make bread—kneading dough works wonders for hot tempers.

➤ Friends—Call a friend and talk, write letters to friends in other cities.

➤ Housework—Yes, housework! Clean, scrub, vacuum, dust, mop, and more as you ventilate angry feelings. Your room will benefit too!

➤ Write—Write down your feelings, then tear up the letter and throw it away. Sometimes just getting the feelings off your chest makes you feel relief.

Communication During Family Conflict

Ask any parent and the one type of communication they most resent is when conflict occurs in the home. *Conflict* may be defined as "a sharp disagreement or opposition, as of interests, ideas," and so forth. And even the most vibrant and caring Christian families experience this from time to time. Sometimes this strife is between parent and child, as with a personality difference. Conflict may also be experienced when members take opposing sides of an issue during a family discussion. And if you are like our family, differences can occur when the kids "team" up against the parents to get their way.

Now usually such conflict is not a major problem. Yet conflict that gets out of hand can be devastating. Barbara and John experienced conflict in their family that almost created a split in their marriage.

"The trouble started with just a few small disagreements each night at dinner. Then Barbara and I began to take sides with the children on mute points," John said. "Finally, before anyone could get control of the issues, I got so disgusted that no one would listen to me, including my wife, that I left the house in anger and didn't come back until late that night."

In our home, it seems the greatest marital conflicts occur when a child plays one parent against the other— without either parent knowing what is going on. For example:

"Mom, can I go to the movie with Joe's parents tonight," our daughter might ask.

"No, you can't. You didn't take out the garbage cans this morning like I asked, and you went to the movie last Friday. Enough is enough," Mom replies.

Okay, our daughter figures. If she won't let me go, I'll ask Dad.

"Dad, can I go to the movie with Joe's parents tonight?" she asks wisely.

"Well, I don't mind," his father replies. "Just be in early. Oh, be sure and tell your mother."

And that is where the parent battle begins. Who is right, and who is wrong? Does she go or does she stay? Another evening of conflict begins due to lack of communication.

Conflict: A Perennial Problem

The conflict we all experience in our families and with friends is nothing new. We can look in the Bible and see that even in the earliest days of the church, people experienced the difficulty of facing conflict and resolving this to find a peaceful solution. Paul affirmed the unity of Christians (even though different in many ways) in Romans 12:5: "We, who are many, are one body in Christ."

Family unity should be the key among Christian parents today. As the leader in the family, you can be instrumental in helping your children to use these conflict situations constructively. These times of difference need not result in hurt feelings or running away. Rather your family can learn to openly discuss the problems and seek workable solutions.

Learning to Live with Diversity

The first step to solving conflict creatively is to listen to all members involved. One friend Jamie said, "I used to blame my oldest daughter for causing all the problems in our family. It never failed—as soon as I turned my back, chaos would break loose between her and her younger twin brothers. Sheila always seemed to be in the middle until one day I noticed the boys teasing and antagonizing Sheila, trying to get her angry. I realized that perhaps she was not the guilty one and began to really hear all sides of the argument."

Avoid making premature judgments before each family member has had a chance to speak. Even then, after hearing all sides of the situation, it helps to answer questions with more questions. Some we use include:

➤ How would you feel if that happened to you?
➤ What do you think a fair solution would be?
➤ How should we solve this as Christians?

Putting the decision on your child keeps you in the position of fair leader and helps your children grow from the conflict as they seek healthy compromise.

Talk openly about the diversified group within the family. Personal preferences can be shown in the length of skirts, color, style of jeans, and the way each member wears his hair. In our home, each person has a different color of hair; not only do we look different, we are different. Personal opinions and viewpoints make it clear that each person in the family thinks differently.

Encourage each member to find his God-given talent and accept this uniqueness as being part of His plan. Then, explain Ephesians 4:4–6, "There is one body and one Spirit, just as you were called in one hope of your calling, one Lord, one faith, one baptism, one God and Father of all." We gather in the Christian family as separate individuals. We experience the faith in many different ways, yet we are united in one body by our belief in one God. Again, family unity is the goal.

Agreeing to Disagree—Positively

In order to control family conflict, each member must agree to disagree in order for personal differences and conflict to turn into group growth. Ted, a father of four, acknowledged, "Before we begin talking about a certain subject at dinnertime, I always ask that we let people express their opinions openly. This is not to say that you must agree or that you must accept any person's opinion as truth. But we need to feel enough love and caring for openness to occur."

Perhaps you and your children are at that stage where you do not agree with each other on any subject. (We have been there and, to be honest, sometimes we are still there!) But as you encourage your children to be open and accepting, and demonstrate these attributes as well, growth will occur.

Of course, even when openness and listening does occur, there will still be arguments. If your clan is like our family, children will bicker over responsibilities, unfair chores, curfews, and even who is touching whom on a family trip. Do these sound familiar?

➤ "I call the front seat. Ashley had it last time."
➤ "I get dibs on the recliner. Brittnye used it yesterday."
➤ "I did the dishes two days ago, and besides, I took out the garbage last week. Rob never does his share."
➤ "Please let me watch just one more show. I promise I'll never watch TV again after tonight. You're letting Brittnye stay up."
➤ "Mom, make Ashley stop looking at me."
➤ "Dad, Rob touched my side of the seat. Do something!"

In the midst of family squabbles (and we've had our share), you can work to keep evaluation and criticism of others positive. For most people criticism causes immediate conflict. Who wants to feel bad inside? When members become critical and sarcastic toward others in the family, the parent has to help the abusers to stay in line. Encourage your children to show empathy before speaking critically by asking: How would I feel if someone said this to me? By encouraging them to reverse the negative statement, a lot of unnecessary harsh words are halted.

The key word to curbing sarcasm in your family is agape, the selfless love that Jesus shared. Such love is in complete opposition to sarcasm and bitterness. Encourage the critical child to think before he or she lashes out with words of judgment. Generally, the insecure member is the most argumentative and critical of others, so spend time developing a caring relationship with this child.

Creative Conflict Resolution

Whatever the source of conflict in your home, creative problem solving is an excellent way of opening doors of compromise. Look at the following steps:

1. State the problem that is troubling the family members.
2. List all of the alternatives at hand. Let your children have fun with this and brainstorm creatively.
3. What are the benefits of each alternative? the disadvantages? What is the worst outcome? the best outcome?
4. Select the choice that meets the most positive needs with the least consequences.
5. Make a decision and try the choice.

In avoiding conflict that leads to disaster, the parent should model positive ways of handling differences. The family members will look up to you for keys in dealing with opposition. Do you quit when your idea is rejected, or do you give your full support to the family? When someone differs with your opinion at home, do you become hostile or do you let others have an opinion too? By seeing you deal with conflict in a positive manner, your children will grow in learning to cope with diversity of opinions.

Conflicts occur in all families, even Christian families. And this conflict does not just go away by itself. You can usually feel the tension brewing in the family before an outburst occurs. Perhaps the conflict began with words said in a joking manner or when one member neglected their responsibilities to the family. The important point to remember is to deal with the conflict before it becomes a hopeless situation. And listen to all sides of the story with an open mind. Finally, constantly affirm that unifying force—God's love— that brings your family together.

During our pilgrimage as a Christian family, at some point we will all take a different road as we follow God's plan for our lives. If each member will walk with love and keep lines of communication open, however, these roads will merge together instead of creating conflict and stumbling blocks among us.

Family Time

1. Use this Anger Check to discuss angry feelings with your child. Discuss how your child handles his anger in these situations.

> My parents criticize my behavior.
> They treat me like my younger brother or sister.
> They are unreasonable with restrictions and limits.
> My siblings invade my privacy.
> My parents don't listen when I want to talk.
> No one takes my feelings and opinions seriously.
> My parents give rules that are too strict.
> My parents criticize my dress and hairstyle.
> My family doesn't like my choices in music and TV shows.
> I resent having to do family chores.
> I feel like my parents favor one child over me.
> My parents are unhappy with my grades and study habits.
> My mom is mad because I don't clean my room.
> My dad is mad because I don't complete my homework.
> My parents are angry because my basketball broke the rose bush in the front yard.

2. During family time, talk about the body language members use to convey a message—laughing eyes, crossed

legs, hands on the hip, tense eyebrows, thumbs up, biting nails, etc. Ask each member to communicate to the family using only body language, and challenge everyone to guess what emotion the member is conveying.

3. During family time, practice the creative conflict resolution as discussed on page 121. Decide on a problem that is of concern to the family, and tell members that "anything goes" as you brainstorm ideas about how to solve this. Follow the following guidelines in your discussion.

A. State a problem that is troubling the family members.

B. List all of the alternatives at hand.

C. What are the benefits of each alternative? The negative repercussions? What is the best outcome? The worst outcome?

D. Select the choice that meets the most positive needs with the least consequences.

E. Make a decision together, and try the choice.

F. Talk about this choice at your next family meeting, and evaluate if it worked as planned.

Notes

1. Ellen Goodman, "For Tsongas and His Family, A Discovery of the Preciousness of Time," *The Boston Globe* (January 17, 1984), with permission.

2. Leo Buscaglia, *Bus 9 to Paradise.* (Thorofare: Flack Inc., 1986), 136–37.

3. William Gottlieb, "The Healthful Art of Listening" *Prevention* (December 1980), 66.

4. Delores Curran, "What Good Parents Are Doing Right," *McCall's* (March 1993), 140.

5. Neala S. Schwartzberg, Ph.D., "That Magic Touch," *Parents* (February 1989), 88.

Chapter 4

Take Control Through Christian Values

America is finally waking up. After spending decades trying to break away from the traditional standards that govern our society and families, we are now realizing that our country is in grave trouble. People have lost respect for the government, for our leaders, for the family, and for each other. Some have also lost respect for the church as it weakens the gospel message and accepts questionable behaviors and principles.

The nineties forecast change for the family with a movement toward commitment, shared goals, personal standards, and high values. Can we honestly take on this massive task?

The Loss of Guiding Principles

Even among Christians, many families today are self-centered rather than Christ-centered. We have been transposed into a "me" generation whose every member seeks what is best for himself or herself. Sacrificing for the benefit of the "whole" has become unheard of, replaced with such statements as "I need to think about what is right for me" or "I'm going to do what makes me happy now." As family members seek self-fulfillment, the concept of oneness has diminished—the very concept early families and our nation was based upon. Instead of gaining strength as one body, the family has become fragile, disjointed and, for many, dysfunctional.

From the covenant relationship God established with Israel, Moses received a set of principles to live by, which we know as the Ten Commandments. These rules offer strength to believers, telling us the distinct difference between right and wrong.

The first four of these commandments deal with our relationship with our Creator.

"I am the LORD, your God, who brought you out of the land of Egypt, out of the house of bondage. You shall have no other gods before me. You shall not make for yourself a graven image. . . . You shall not take the name of the LORD your God in vain. . . . Observe the sabbath day to keep it holy" (Deut. 5:6–11, RSV).

The remaining six commandments deal with our relationship with others:

"Honor your father and mother. . . . You shall not kill. Neither shall you commit adultery. Neither shall you steal. Neither shall you bear false witness against your neighbor. Neither shall you covet" (Deut. 5:16–21).

The Ten Commandments—ten rules of human conduct and eternal guiding principles. But how often are these rules ridiculed and ignored! Perhaps the loss of these standards in our society is at the root of our moral decline. The eternal principles reflect the presence of God in our life. A few years ago when the theologians said that God is dead, they meant that God had lost His place of importance in our life as a society. We turn to medical doctors when we are sick, psychologists when we are fearful, prominent role models when we desire to know about right behavior. Where does God make any difference in our lives today?

With the loss of these divine foundations has come a blurring of what is right and wrong, acceptable and unacceptable, appropriate and inappropriate. Thus, many people wander in a moral and spiritual fog. The sad result is not freedom, but slavery.

A story is told of some psychologists who thought that the fences around the playgrounds of children were negative influences. So they took down the fences and gave the children total freedom—no boundaries, no fences. But an interesting result happened. When the fences were removed, the children did not run the length and breadth of the playground the way they used to. Instead, they huddled in the middle of the playground and demonstrated behavior indicating intense feelings of insecurity. As soon as the fences were replaced, their feelings of security and freedom were renewed. God's children of all ages need limits and boundaries; we must have rules to live by.

In order for us to reclaim the cherished and compassionate values from days past, we must begin to model and teach these at home. Children are not born knowing right from wrong; these personal standards, including morals, ethical behavior, and empathy, must be taught as we tell our children what we believe.

Just What Are Values?

Values are the emotional rules by which a nation governs itself. Values summarize the accumulated folk wisdom by which a society organizes and disciplines itself. And values are the precious reminders that individuals obey to bring order and meaning into their personal lives.[1]

Experts used to feel that if children grew up in a two-parent family, they would naturally grow up with high values. But today we know that there are no guarantees unless a conscious effort is made to pass on the very quintessence of a moral culture. Having a certain type of family—two parents or one, blended, or something else—is not an acid test for good family living. "We've never held up one particular family as the model," said Wayne Scott, president of the American Family Association. "That, to me, is not the core of it. It's more a matter of principles that people live by."

Scott encourages people to practice traditional ethical values like honesty, monogamy, and commitment to family members. He said those values "have stood the test of time for centuries," but are not practiced regularly enough.[2]

The family provides our first understanding of traditional ethical values, providing a safe "testing ground" for children. Within the nest of this accepting group of people, the child can experiment with all sorts of rebellious behavior, testing to see what will be approved and what will be disapproved. Parents who spend time daily teaching children morals and personal standards are rewarded as the child goes into the world with strong character and benevolence toward others. When children learn at home how to resolve conflict without physical violence, how to treat others compassionately, and how to choose right over wrong, they take these treasured behaviors into the school and neighborhood and then ultimately into their families and society. Society as a whole, and our nation in particular, will benefit if we can reclaim the meaning of family by teaching the highest values at home.

Your Child's First Teacher

Values, a quality we can not see and certainly find difficult to define, are communicated most powerfully by parents. Though a child's friends may be influential, their power usually emerges as dominant only if their relationship of love and caring with parents is broken or vastly diminished. The prime communicator of values is still the parents.[3]

Teaching morals and values to children is not an easy task these days, however. In the past, schools and churches played a key role in fostering moral development. Now, with religious influence in decline and schools wavering over the way to teach values, parents are basically on their own. Other recent social trends have complicated the transmission of values. "We're raising a generation that is still groping for a good future direction," says psychologist William Damon, head of Brown University's education department. Many of today's parents were raised in the sixties, the age of permissiveness, and their children were born in the age of affluence in the eighties, when materialism was rampant. "It's an unholy combination," says Damon.[4]

The family is the child's very first and most important teacher when it comes to issues of morality and personal standards. After all, parents have years of experience and wisdom to know what is right and just in the world, and, ideally, values are taught by parents telling children what is acceptable in life. Children then can model their lives after the parent. The child who learns at home that it is wrong to hit others or take things that are not his, will go into the world—at school or play—and display this correct behavior. Likewise, a child who is taught at home that calling people names, disrespecting authority, and lying are not acceptable will remember this and act responsibly in public places. From the family children learn to be benevolent to those in need, to show compassion when someone is hurting, and to reach out in love to those who need to know the acceptance of our Lord Jesus Christ.

As Christian parents, we have opportunities each day to listen, build up, and teach biblical truths. We can guide our children to view life with hope and optimism, and encourage our children to become the best they can be. Remember, however, that what we think each day, how we act and react to parenting situations, and what we say to those around us—all govern our overall perspective on life. Parenting expectations and attitude determine the path your child will take. As you become more aware of the attributes of being a positive parent, you can interpret these techniques into your lifestyle.

Boost Your Child's Self-Esteem

In order to stand strong for the personal standards you teach, your children must feel secure with positive self-esteem. Self-esteem is a child's feeling about himself and the basis of his respect for self and others.

What you say to your child has a tremendous influence on his or her life and our developing self-esteem. Your thoughts, feelings, and behavior mirror your soul—if you are full of depressing thoughts, doubts, and suspicions regarding your child, then his attitude toward life becomes negative. If you are enthusiastic, hopeful, and positive, your parenting skills can be filled with meaning and have a vibrant impression on your children.

Building a child's self-esteem begins at the moment of birth; some research even suggests that it may begin in the prenatal environment. The way we hold, cuddle, speak to, and meet the needs of that tiny infant is a determining factor in how he will feel about himself.

Children need a healthy sense of self-worth to relate in their expanding world. As soon as they begin to interact with peers, they will be challenged. A person's total being, outlook on life, and choice of friends depend to a large extent on his self-concept. This pride or respect to ward off society's evils develops as a child feels worthwhile to the family—loveable, and capable.

Children with high self-esteem are less likely to abuse drugs and alcohol, have early sexual experiences, or follow the crowd; they have a strong inner confidence that allows them to stand strong for the personal standards they believe in.

Nurture Your Children

You can boost your child's self-concept through many daily activities. Children with a positive self-concept need someone— a parent—who believes in them unconditionally, similar to God's love for us. They have adults who nurture them with praise, hugs, and discipline; who comfort them when they fail; and who then push them out the door to try again and again.

The ability to nurture is not an option: it is essential if you want to raise healthy children. In essence, nurturing is the spiritual quality of parenthood, the undefinable element that separates the good from the bad and the adequate from the inadequate.

What is the magical quality called nurturance? It's the instinct to provide comfort when your child is sick, to soothe her when she is frightened. Those parents who nurture best do a lot of touching and kissing, and while their children may feign embarrassment, those kids are the ones who are the most secure—the learners, the leaders.[5]

Nurture and affirmation are necessary ingredients to encourage self-esteem. Consider the following statements you can say to your children each day no matter how negative the situation may be:

➤ "Good job!"
➤ "Keep up the good work."
➤ "That is an interesting thought."
➤ "I appreciate your . . . (thoughtfulness, help, caring)."
➤ "I love being your parent. You make my day special."

Parents can also help a child gain the strong weapon of self-confidence through hugs—even when that parent is angry. Often a loving touch enables you to be sensitive in situations where words seem out of place. You can do this by offering those extra strokes and hugs even when the child is not too lovable. A pat on the shoulder, a hug, a firm handshake, or other strokes usually generate a stronger sense of caring and concern than spoken words. This touching breaks down barriers and says, "I care about you."

Give your child situations that promise success, for as a child experiences these small achievements, he will gain confidence and an attitude of value. Whether it involves having the child become Mom's super-helper during dinnertime or Dad's handy assistant on Saturdays, think of ways that your child can experience success and then praise him or her for this.

Praise the little accomplishments your child makes—no matter how small they may be. As a child begins to feel competent and confident, he or she will attack greater tasks with a sense of power. If your child cries for help while tackling a project, offer support and words of encouragement, but let him or her become independent and gain the necessary confidence of a strong individual.

Appreciation Tips

Take time each day to let your child know of your love and belief in him or her. The following ways let your child know he is acceptable to you and help to boost self-esteem:

➤ Write a love note. Sometimes a parent's spoken word is ignored by children, but a love note placed on the child's bed may be appropriate communication. Use this love note to say, "I'm sorry," "I'm proud of you," or simply "I love you."

➤ Buy ingredients for a special dessert and make it together. It's Friday night, and everyone in the family has plans—except your child. Have a supply of ingredients to make chocolate chip cookies or rich fudge brownies, turn up the music, and make something outrageously yummy with them. Be sure to lick the bowl as you enjoy a time of parent-child bonding.

➤ Affirm your child's accomplishments. A handwritten banner hung across his or her bed, a note on the refrigerator, or a colorful balloon tied to the mailbox are all ways to affirm your child's special accomplishments. From an improved grade on a test to winning a school election to waking up in a good mood for a week, parents have opportunities everyday to celebrate victories.

➤ Tell someone about your child's accomplishments. Everyone likes to hear words of affirmation. Tell another adult—a neighbor or a grandparent—how great your child is, while he or she is within listening distance. While your child may appear modest, these words of affirmation will last a long time.

➤ Put a note in your child's lunch. Especially after a rushed morning, notes in the lunch bag that say "You are special" are meaningful to any child.

Develop Empathy and Tolerance

A child who maintains high morals and personal standards needs to develop tolerance for others. As you show consideration for others, your child will model your attitude toward his or her peers. Realize that each child develops at his own pace and is made in God's image. Talk with your child about his or her uniqueness and how God wants us to accept all His people—especially those who are different.

Empathy involves caring for someone else to the point that you know how they feel, leading to altruism. When we really feel what someone is going through, we want to reach out to them and help them. Children learn to have empathy as parents give emotional feedback by either showing pleasure or displeasure to their actions or speech.

When our daughter decided not to play with her friend because she still spoke "baby talk," we knew it was time to discuss the situation. Watch for signs that demonstrate that your child is not accepting peers. Talk openly about the potential in all of God's children, and observe your child at play to make sure the rules of tolerance are being followed. We have leaned on the phrase, "How would you feel if someone did that to you?" to encourage acceptance of all God's people. Once a child can react with empathy toward others, you can feel assured that the message of high values is being carried out into his or her world.

You can develop a child's ability to empathize with others through daily experiences. As your child interacts with others and experiences conflict, ask:

➤ "What made you want to do that?"
➤ "What if someone did that to you?"
➤ "How would that make you feel?"
➤ "How would you want a friend to treat you?"
➤ "Would your feelings then change?"
➤ "What can you do to apologize to your friend?"

You can help teach these values by role playing situations with your child. Create a situation that may not be fair or that may be unkind, and let your child discuss how he or she would act. When we were growing up, a popular children's magazine had a regular cartoon series that depicted two boys with contrasting behaviors and attitudes. One boy responded appropriately, while the other boy acted in rebellion and anger. Children can identify with both individuals, but the family must encourage the correct way to treat others.

If your child acts like a bully around others, respond immediately. No one should be allowed to put someone else down—for any reason. If you need to punish your child for such behavior, do so, and then talk openly about how that person must have felt. Get the message across that God's plan for the world includes acceptance, compassion, and loving our neighbors as we love ourselves.

Spend Time Together

Have you spent time alone with your children recently? Would your family relationship profit from time together in a quiet, relaxed atmosphere? Use this together time to rediscover each family member's gifts, talents, dreams, and fears. Only by spending quiet time together without the distraction of the world around you can personal standards be shared.

A child will learn the highest morals and values by watching you act and react in the world. The ways you care for others set an important pattern that the children will slowly recognize and establish in their own lives. How you handle neighbor relationships, family matters, and community involvement reinforces the priorities that you have spoken of as being important in your life.

Let your child know through simple conversation that you are human and have feelings, just as he does. Tell them what God is doing in your own life, and help him to see your own Christian standards by discussing the priorities in your life. Help him to understand why you took supper to the neighbor's house when there was a death in the family; why you did the laundry of an ill friend; why you volunteer your time to build houses for the needy; why you donate canned goods for Thanksgiving and Christmas baskets, and so on. Talk to him about the importance of family—caring for elderly relatives and keeping in touch with members who live far away.

Remember the old saying: Watch what you do, because they (children) watch what you do. Many times, more values are caught while children observe parents in action through daily living than are taught by mere words. Put your words and actions together to ensure the highest family values in your home.

Teach Honesty

Psychologists tell us that people who are secure and happy with themselves have no need to humiliate others. On the contrary, a sign of security and maturity is the ability to develop a positive relationship in which there is mutual support. There is a big difference between positive critique and negative criticism. Honesty is certainly an important element in positive relationships, but how and why honest words are spoken is just as important.

You can teach your children to temper honest communication with tact. Tact is that delicate perception of knowing the right thing to say or do without offending the other person. When a person uses tact in talking with others—without distorting the truth in any way—growth can occur. You use tact in a relationship because you care about the other person and how he or she feels. This involves speaking the truth with hopes of preserving the friendship rather than tearing it apart.

According to Ms. Charlotte Sotak, M.S.Ed., NCC, honesty plays a vital role in every relationship, but so does tactfulness. "We turn to our friends for honest answers, trusting them and their opinions," Sotak, a counselor in the public school system, said. "Our friends can support and help validate our goals, helping us grow in self-esteem and self-confidence."

"But there are times that the job of a friend is to point out errors, poor judgment, or negative behavior. How we present this to the offending person takes much thought and a careful delivery. A blunt, direct attack only causes one to recoil and reject the advice. This hurts and causes the offender to miss the message which might be important and 'right on target.'"

The Bible has much to add to speaking the truth with tact. In Ephesians 4:15 (RSV) we read "speaking the truth in love."

Also in Ephesians 4:25 (RSV) we find "putting away falsehood, let everyone speak the truth." In Philippians 4:8 Paul also teaches, "Finally, brethren, whatever is true, whatever is honorable, whatever is right, whatever is pure, whatever is lovely, whatever is of good repute, if there is any excellence and if anything worthy of praise, let your mind dwell on these things."

In the Gospels, Jesus teaches us a lifestyle full of empathy, of being sensitive to those around us. This *agape* or selfless love enables us to meet the personal needs of our family and friends, rather than tearing people down.[6]

Develop Moral Behavior

Paul offered this observation in his letter to the Corinthians: "When I was a child, I used to speak as a child, think as a child and reason as a child; when I became a man, I did away with childish things" (1 Cor. 13:11).

"It would be a lot easier if kids were born knowing right from wrong," Luci said as she put four-year-old Kevin in time-out for the fourth time that day. "He has tested every limit imposed on him—taking toys from his friend, pushing his sister, kicking the dog, and screaming at me. When will it ever end?"

If you have a four-year-old, you might wonder the same question—when will it ever end? The irony is that the parent of a hormonal fourteen-year-old might be asking the same question! And the exhausting truth is this—parenting never ends. The parent who wants to see the child grow up into a moral young adult must continually teach this behavior in the home. Now, do not close the book yet. . . .

Moral behavior involves treating others the way we would want to be treated or in laymen's terms—following the Golden Rule. We recall our son at age seven, sitting in time-out. "Doesn't that rule say do unto others the way they do to you?"

he asked angrily after punching his friend in the back. "Well, he pushed me first."

Beginning at the age of five or six, children become capable of recognizing the difference between an intentional wrongdoing and an accidental wrongdoing. They become capable of making a choice guided by an understanding of what is right or wrong. Many psychologists believe there are two pathways for this moral growth to proceed: first, by identification with a moral parent; and second, by fearing loss of love or parental support.

The child who identifies with a moral parent and is taught by the use of loving limits is more likely to internalize moral standards, rather than just acting out of fear.[7]

Model Agape or Self-less Love

Helping children learn this rule for human moral behavior is not easy, but it can be taught as you model the *agape* love of Jesus. This type of love is not self-serving, but it focuses on the needs of others. It intends to minister to others in a manner that will meet their needs. And in a selfish, "gimme" society, it is a most difficult type of love to share.

Moral behavior has two components: Its intention must be good, in the sense that its goal is the well-being of one or more people; and it must be fair or just, in the sense that it considers the rights of others without prejudice or favoritism. Helping my friend gain an unwarranted advantage over others may be kind to him but it is not fair, and thus not an instance of moral behavior. Treating everybody cruelly may be fair, but it is not kind, and therefore, it is not moral. Conversely, we consider an act immoral if it seeks to harm others or gain an unfair advantage over them. A person's acts may be moral, immoral, or amoral—the last referring to behavior not performed specifically to benefit or harm others.[8]

Psychologist Lawrence Kohlberg identified stages of children as they mature into adolescence, then into adulthood.

These stages begin at birth and progress as the child grows in years and maturity. A child may try to avoid punishment at ages two to six, do tradeoffs with others (if you'll be nice; I'll be nice) at ages six to ten, believe fully in law and order at ages eleven to fifteen, then begin to understand Democracy and conscience at fourteen years on up. [9]

The reason for understanding these stages is not to say that children are locked into a certain pattern at one age. If that were the case, then parents would have no responsibility to encourage moral development. What is important is that our minds develop in a progression according to God's plan.

You may feel that your child is "not getting the picture" as you talk about right and wrong, loving others, and making moral decisions; but if you realize the stages of development a child must pass through, you can confidently keep on teaching the highest values. What you are teaching will sink in—maybe not today or tomorrow, but in God's time. Only by struggling with daily decisions and encounters with peers and adults will your child assimilate this moral knowledge and sense of truth and falsehood and grow into mature Christian adulthood.

Be in the World, Not of the World

As Christians, we are called to live in the world, but not be of the world. We can experience an abundant life right where we are without giving in to demands that tear at our moral beliefs. What demands are made on families today? The list is extensive:

➤ School and extracurricular activities that conflict with family times
➤ Neighbors and friends with different moral behavior
➤ Contradicting and secular values from children at school
➤ Adult teachers and leaders whose personal standards differ drastically from those taught at home

> Opinions given in classrooms that are inconsistent with Christian beliefs
> Media stories that project decaying values
> Church leaders who may not be answering God's call
> Advertising that glamorizes alcohol, cigarettes, and promiscuity

Parents, Stand Firm

Because we are living in such a free and diverse society where everyone can speak their mind, our children are faced with forces at school, work, and play that greatly oppose the values and morals taught at home. Knowing this, you can handle these outside influences in a way that is open and supportive.

Encourage Openness with Your Child

Talk about the opposing situation, whether it is a teacher who is espousing opposing values, a coach who is being too aggressive, or a news story that is sexually suggestive and portrays women or men in a negative manner. Parents can give strength and reassurance as children share their feelings of intolerance or anger. Empathy and caring can take place as these concerns and feelings are expressed.

When your family's values are challenged, use the situation to clarify what your family believes and to explain why these personal standards are significant to the family. Many families never talk about why they believe in what they do—until someone challenges them or until a child goes astray. Use everyday situations to explain right and wrong to your child, and give them strong protection to face an oppositional world.

Know When to Draw the Line

Parents must talk about their values and goals in order for changes to take place. And parents today must decide when to draw the line as outside influences interrupt family time or interfere with family values. If the outside influence is affecting your family, you may choose to place your child in another class or change activities to get away from the dissension. Remember, you set the rules and limits for your family, not the school or society.

Continue Living in the World

Facing a world with opposing values and morals is very difficult for Christian families today, especially with the pressure young people feel to follow the crowd. Your child may feel as if his or her world has collapsed when you say no to an activity or questionable influence. Yet God gives strength to begin anew. Fellowship and communication within the family are vital, for strength can come from within this tight-knit unit.

Tell your child about times when you felt challenged and how you handled it. These recollections could be when you were a teen or an adult. Your child must know that standing strong for what he or she believes is an honorable attribute and adds to character and integrity.

Forgive the Opposing Influence

The whole principle of the gospel lies in loving and forgiving. Often, however, as we harbor feelings of anguish after an outside influence has intruded on family values, forgiveness is difficult. By placing our faith in God and by building our lives around His Word through continual prayer, fellowship, and service, we can experience the strength to forgive those who are different or who have different standards. Agape or selfless love becomes a reality as we generate acceptance, forgiveness, and growth, and as we place our ultimate faith in God instead of humankind. We always tell our children—

➤ "Everyone else may feel this is true, but we believe this in our family."
➤ "Your teacher may feel that way, but we feel this way."
➤ "They might let their children go there, but we don't feel it is right."
➤ "She might wear clothes like that, but in our family, we don't do that."
➤ "He may be allowed to watch that television show, but we don't like the message it sends."
➤ "The advertisement may look enticing, but we know it is unhealthy (or wrong)."

It is important for your child to learn acceptance when outside influences interfere with family rules. The idea of loving the person, but disagreeing with what they do or say is significant for your child as he learns to live in the world as a follower of Christ.

The Scriptures never promised that our lives would be easy. But God's Word does offer acceptance, loving forgiveness, and strength to cope during times of opposing influences.

Is It Ever Too Late?

Every family must have a code of ethics to live by. If you have ignored giving this code to your children for whatever reason, it is never too late to start teaching ethics, morals, and high personal standards.

It will be difficult to change already formed behaviors, especially if your children are used to following the crowd or learning their values from others, whether teachers, friends, or coaches. But with family meetings to discuss what you believe, personal one-on-one discussions with your child, rewarding moral behavior, and reprimanding unsuitable behavior—and much prayer—you can start on the path to establishing family values in your home.

Everyone's Not Doing It

To watch the popular television shows such as "Beverly Hills, 90210," "Doogie Houser, M.D.," "and Roseanne," one would assume from the promiscuous portrayal of teen behavior that everyone's having sex today.

Well, contrary to popular opinion, everyone's not doing it. Perhaps it is the fear of getting pregnant, the death sentence of AIDS, or maybe America is finally waking up to a resurgence of morals and values, but many teens across the nation are saying no to promiscuity and yes to sexual abstinence before marriage.

Sexuality: Hurried to Grow Up

Thirty years ago, parents took pride in protecting children from growing up too fast, holding them back from conversations and suggestions that were too "adult." Many parents would say, "We don't discuss that in our family." But sadly enough, today's parents are forced to prevent children from the perils of a fast-paced, hurried society with weakened morals and values. Sex is a mandatory discussion in most homes, not to encourage children to become active, but to alert them to the many hazards life has in store—if they break the rules.

When our three teens were in sixth grade, they took an abstinence-based sex education course through the public schools. This course discussed the anatomy and physiology of men and women, human reproduction, society's standards, and abstinence. At that age it was easy to talk with our children about sex.

But as our children became teenagers, suddenly the openness ended. That is when we made a conscious effort to educate our teens about sex while affirming our Christian beliefs.

Have Age-Appropriate Discussions

Parents ask: When is the appropriate time to talk with children about sexual behavior? Yesterday! If you are not open about sex, it will be difficult to break the ice. To make certain your child understands your values, this communication must be open. In other words, you must be able to say the word *sex* without trembling!

Start at a Young Age. A child's favorite teacher is the parent. When you teach your children about sexuality, you can express your values before they hear differing opinions from others. It is much easier if you begin talking when your child is a toddler and preschooler. If your child never asks questions, initiate the discussion. You might say, "Aunt Susan is now pregnant," and explain what this means. Answer questions honestly and briefly, but use appropriate language for the child's age. Expect to be uncomfortable with your child and admit this, if necessary. It will get easier as you get used to talking about a subject that was "taboo" when you were a child. Remember, sex is a natural part of life. If we feel dirty or wrong when talking about this with our children, we will pass on to them the wrong ideas.

Be accessible to your children, and answer their questions. Talk to them about how they were born—tell them when it was, where it was, how you and your spouse felt at that time, the names that were picked out, and more. Let them know who came to visit, what gifts they received, and show them pictures you took. This all gives children a sense of family and connectedness.

By age two, most children recognize the differences between boys and girls and begin to establish gender identities. By age four, most children become interested in babies and the birth process. Parents are often uncomfortable and unsure how to respond to questions about conception and birth. When discussing these topics, children tend to interpret information given in a literal manner. For example, one child thought she was bought in a store and then "hatched," after being told she came from an egg inside her mother.

During kindergarten age, a decrease in sexual play is seen and an increase in modesty develops. New words and terminology are learned by telling jokes, singing songs, or repeating rhymes learned from older children. You do not have to give full details when discussing sex at this age which would present more than the child can understand. Be age-appropriate as you address the question without bringing up other related subjects.[10]

Early elementary age. Children's understanding of sex and childbirth changes greatly between the ages of six and nine. Six year olds are still egocentric thinkers, with personal opinions about how things work. They may reject the facts of life in favor of their own ideas about sex. Eight and nine-year-olds can accept others' thoughts and are better able to understand sex and birth.[11] By this age, if a child has not initiated discussions about sex or asked "why," parents need to begin with the facts.

Listen carefully to your child's concerns at this age. Offer your explanations, and see how much your child knows about sex. Include discussions about human emotions and values in addition to the biological facts of life. Because younger children are much more receptive to a parent's personal values than teenagers are, discuss puberty early before the child experiences physical changes. Physical changes occur before age ten for many children today. Let children know what is going to happen to their bodies, but also let them know how you feel about sexual behaviors.

The Teenage Years. By the teenage years most children have a great understanding of sexuality, but they may have learned this from a friend, MTV, or the latest teen magazine. Do they understand the Christian's perspective? A twelve-year-old boy may suddenly become enthralled with the bathing suit photographs in a sports magazine; a fourteen-year-old girl may bring home teen magazines from the drugstore with articles on how to flirt, dating, and sexual relationships. But reading secular articles on sex and dating or looking at an advertiser's portrayal of love does not convey a Christian view of sexuality.

In our family, discussions about sex from a Christian perspective began at an early age with a constant exchange of ideas. When our children were in elementary school, they asked us questions about sexual behavior, and we answered the questions honestly but also interjected statements such as, "In our home, we feel that is wrong" or "As Christians, we feel that sex is saved for marriage." If we saw our children looking at sexually candid billboards or television commercials, we spoke openly about what they were seeing and added our personal beliefs. Rather than giving a negative impression about sexuality, we affirmed the beauty of sex as having God's blessings in the context of marriage. Moral training was incorporated into our daily lifestyle and conversation.

By the age of twelve, teens should know the facts about sex and how this will affect them as they go through puberty. But also by this age teens should know, from their parents the facts about the family's values.

Talk openly with your teen about sexual feelings, and emphasize Christian beliefs about abstinence until marriage. Let your older teen know what he or she will be faced with when they begin dating, and help him work through personal values and find ways of saying no to aggressive dates. Talk with your older teen about how to treat a date, with respect and courtesy.

Teach Self-Control, Not Birth Control

The National Center for Health Statistics data on out-of-wedlock childbearing reported that in 1991, nearly 30 percent of all newborns came home from the hospital with a mother who was not married to the father. In the 1980s alone, out-of-wedlock births swelled by an astonishing 32 percent.[12]

Do not let your child become part of this rising group of "babies having babies." Talk with your teen about sex and emphasize self-control along with Christian values. Children should grow up knowing the Christian's response to premarital sex. Tell your children how you feel, and stand proudly for your belief. Let your teen know that he or she is in charge of their body. We emphasize the following in our home:

➤ God planned for sex within the context of marriage. He expects the highest morals from all of us and does not accept lustful behavior.

➤ We have the highest dreams for you. We want you to go to college, learn a trade, fulfill your goals, and use your talents. We want the best for you and want you to avoid the harmful consequences of premarital sex.

➤ The cost of sex before marriage is high. From AIDS and other sexually transmitted diseases to pregnancy—these don't have to be concerns for you if you say "no" to premarital sex.

We recommend the following Scriptures to open discussion with your teen on a Christian's perspective of sex.

➤ God created sex (Gen. 2:18–22; Ps. 139:13).
➤ God has a plan for sex (Matt. 19: 4–6; Gen. 2:24).
➤ God gives instructions on sexuality (Heb. 13:4; Gal. 5: 19–20).
➤ God has two reasons to wait (Deut. 10:12–13; Jer. 29:11).

What About Sex Education?

Sex education in the schools can be an excellent supplement to a parent's teachings at home—if it is abstinence-based. Our local school board has adopted an abstinence-based curriculum which complements our moral beliefs at home, that sex is to be saved for marriage.

It is important to know what your school is teaching. Ask to read through the curriculum, and attend any parent meetings where they highlight the values taught. You must decide if the curriculum is following the high standards you have at home or if it is contradictory to your family values.

Telling Your Child About AIDS

Every child has the right to know about the AIDS virus—how it is transmitted and its devastating effects. If your child ever listens to the evening news, the term AIDS is nothing new. As you talk with your older child, find out what he or she knows before you give the facts. You can then tell your child that AIDS is a deadly disease that is passed to others through sex and needles, but there are ways to prevent it from happening to you.

As your child matures, you can add information on prevention according to the child's maturity. For the teenager, the best AIDS prevention is abstinence and refusing to use drugs. Make sure your child understands the ground rules so he does not live with the anxiety of getting this virus.

If Not from You, Then from Who?

If you listen to the lyrics of popular rock songs or watch the videos on MTV, then you must be aware that sexual promiscuity is often encouraged. But who said that your teen must get his values from these places?

If you have no television or movie rules, set some today. Be aware of the messages your teen is being exposed to. Tell your teen he or she cannot watch a particular show or R-rated movie because the values being presented are not consistent with yours.

If you hear your teen listening to music that has sexually explicit lyrics, talk openly about them. We have found that teens do get embarrassed when parents talk about the words, but they also do hear you. We have confiscated several CDs and tapes with lyrics we do not approve and filed these in the garbage.

With Freedom Comes Responsibility

The most important point you can emphasize with your teen is that with sexual freedom comes adult responsibility. In our family at some point, all of our teens have clearly expressed that they are not ready to give up what they would have to take on this responsibility.

For teens who are college-bound or who look forward to starting an exciting career after high school, having an un-wanted pregnancy or sexually transmitted disease would put a halt to all their life dreams.

Openness Is the Key

You may talk forever to your older teen, yet he or she may rarely acknowledge what you say. But keep talking about sexuality and your personal standards. Teens do hear you and do use this information to form their own beliefs.

What About Drugs and Alcohol?

A recent study by the University of Michigan shows that smoking and drug use by teenagers in America are increasing after a decade of decline. Lloyd Johnston, who directed the study, said, "With more young people smoking cigarettes and smoking marijuana, and with the psychological and social constraints on use declining, the stage is set for a potential resurgence of cocaine and crack use in this population."[13]

You can scream, yell, and forbid your teen not to use drugs or alcohol, but you will not be with them when decisions are made. Usually this decision is made in a room filled with laughing, insecure peers who are ready to try anything to prove their invincibility. Even if your child has always been the "good, moral kid," he will most likely be tempted to try drugs or alcohol at some point during the teenage years. Parents can help their teens resist this temptation:

1. Become educated about drug and alcohol use. Tell your teens the facts: alcohol is illegal for persons underage and drugs are illegal and harmful for anyone. Talk with your teen, using pamphlets on the hazards of substance abuse. Make sure your young person knows the rules of your home as well as the legal system and the repercussions of breaking these laws. Too often well-meaning parents take a comfortable approach to the problem of drug and alcohol use by teenagers, saying, "My kid is active in the anti-drug campaign at school. It can't happen to my child." Often these are the very teens that get caught in the act. Treat substance abuse as you would any other area of living, setting rules that are firm in your family. Do not use anyone's else rules; do what is right for your home. Say "no" and mean it.

2. Talk about choices. Emphasize to your teen that good choices have positive results, and bad choices have negative results. Every choice we take in life has a consequence—good or bad. Our hope and courage comes from God, who promises that as we are in relationship with Him, He will give us wisdom and strength to make the best choices. You cannot overemphasize making wise choices with impulsive teenagers who often forget who they are when they are around peers.

3. Talk about the personal Christian standards your family has. Let your child know that your family is special and has pride in its values and morals. If personal standards are taught at a young age, your communication during the teenage years reinforces this teaching. If the teen does stray and is tempted by drugs or alcohol, they usually come back to the family ideals if standards have been emphasized.

4. Keep open communication in your home. Let your teen know she can talk with you before she has a problem. Being approachable means not lecturing when the teen discusses the sensitive subjects such as drug and alcohol abuse. Let the teen air her views; then offer her your opinion in love.

Tell your teen how substance abuse can make him lose control of his senses—his minds, his coordination, his reasoning—and let him know how you feel personally. We have found it also helps to give our teens answers they can use when peer pressure makes it difficult to say no. Often knowing a quick response saves the teen from making a mistake when under pressure:

➤ "Sorry, I'm allergic to smoke."
➤ "Sorry, I'm allergic to alcohol."
➤ "I can't. I'm taking medicine right now."
➤ "Sorry, alcohol makes me too nervous."
➤ "Not today. I'm not in the mood."
➤ "Sorry. This isn't something I want to do."
➤ "My parents are hysterics. They smell my breath when I get home."
➤ "I'm into health and fitness. That doesn't fit my routine."
➤ "My parents are so strict that they will ground me for even thinking about alcohol (drugs)."
➤ "Sorry, I'm the designated driver tonight (and tomorrow night and the next night)."

This does not give your teen permission to lie; however, when peers put on pressure, your teen needs to know exactly what to say—ahead of time. For some teens, practicing these statements gives them more strength than just saying no and prevents them from being talked into something they really do not want to do anyway.

5. Be an active family unit. Plan activities for your teen and his friends. Encourage the gang to come to your house

and provide a place for the youth to sit, talk, play, and just "be." Boredom encourages substance abuse, and this is where the caring family can help. While your child's friends are at your house, tell them how you feel about drugs and alcohol.

Many parents have not spent time giving teens correct information, and you might reach a child who needs answers. In our home, we have been called "the gestapo parents" laughingly by our teens' friends. But for some reason, our home represents safety as teens congregate here for videos and food on weekend nights. It is okay to be strong about the values you believe in; it is okay to share these with your teen and his friends.

6. Get to know your child's friends. Become interested in their music, activities, and sports events. Watch for symptoms that may surface from a companion who may not be suitable for your teen. If you receive proof that the companion is a negative influence, discuss your feelings and fears openly with your child. Express your reasons for not wanting the child to associate with the friend and stand firm in your demands.

Especially during the teen years when peers are vital to their feelings of security, your child still needs guidance in choosing responsible friends. A youth counselor with a government agency in our town commented, "It is usually the young person whose parents are too busy to know where he is or to care about him who is in trouble with drugs and alcohol." The teen years are your last chance to give your child a healthy start into responsible adulthood.

7. Establish rules before your teen goes out with anyone. Before our teens can leave the house, they must answer the following questions:

➤ Where are you going (phone number and address)?
➤ How are you getting there?
➤ Whom are you going with?
➤ Who will be driving?

➤ Who will be meeting you there?

➤ Will an adult be present? Who is this person?

➤ What time will you be leaving?

➤ When will you arrive home?

➤ If someone has drugs or alcohol, will you leave immediately?

➤ Will you call us if the driver drinks?

Our teens have learned, through trial and error, to obey the family rules in order to have the freedom to go again the next weekend. To be quite honest, spending several weekends watching home videos with Mom and Dad will encourage any teen to abide by the family rules! These rules are set for one main reason—to protect the child.

While teenagers see the rules as being limiting, they will eventually respect your reasons if you keep communication open. Also let your teen know the consequences should they break the rules, such as "if you drink, you will be grounded for a lengthy period of time," or "if we call the party and you are not there, you will be staying home for awhile." Our teens always ask, "How will you find out if we break the rules?" But they also know that being the type of parents we are, we do and will find out!

Let your teen know that trust is very difficult to regain once it has been broken. When they break the family's rules, it will take weeks, maybe months, before you can trust them to be independent again.

8. Stay in the church. As you attend church with your teen, you can experience a special bond between parent and child. Not only will the young person grow from the biblical teachings, but he will also see you and other adults as Christ-like role models.

9. Do not use alcohol and illegal drugs yourself, and do not keep them in your home. This is as important as anything you say. Young people will respect parents who send the

message: "Do as I do" instead of merely "Do as I say." The best way to encourage a drug-free child is to be drug-free yourself.

10. Become an advocate for forgiveness. If your child does experiment with drugs or alcohol, use the situation as an opportunity to get help for your child and to unite as a family. Many teens will continue to test your message to see if what you are saying is really true—simply because they are children. Accepting and loving those who have committed wrongdoings is what our Lord preached and lived. As Christian parents, we are to carry this message of unconditional love and forgiveness to those in our homes.

Drug and alcohol abuse is a problem that is becoming more common with each day, even among the youngest teens. As a caring parent, you can strengthen your teen's values and personal standards as you care enough to provide education, Christian fellowship, and a close relationship with Jesus Christ in your home.

Celebrate Family

In our fragmented society, it is important to teach our children that "family" is important. Grandparents, aunts, uncles, and cousins are all part of our extended family, and this relationship must be nurtured and encouraged in order to blossom. As families relocate across the nation and start new lives, ties that were once strong weaken. As you reclaim the family values so important to strengthen the home, lean on your past for meaning and purpose in life.

The Importance of Family Heritage

With each of us, our roots are firmly planted in the past; therefore, we should all try to discover and preserve our family history. You can start by documenting what you know about yourself and your immediate family, and then you can ask questions of older relatives. Try to find out important names, dates, places, and relationships pertaining to your family. Some relatives may have already collected this information and have it saved.

In your search for history, collect old family Bibles, photo albums, pictures, letters, diaries, church records, legal papers. Do not forget the importance of family cemeteries; those markers offer valuable information about our past.

Family Statistics

Birth and death registrations became a requirement about the turn of the century (1890–1915). Also, deeds, wills, military records, tax forms, social security information, citizenship papers, and health records may be found in local court houses in most cities. If you request copies of these records, be sure to specify dates and names. Include a stamped, self-addressed envelope and offer to pay for the research.

Local libraries in your family's hometown offer many useful sources of information, including the history of the area, location maps, old newspapers, and books on genealogy.

Plan an Annual Family Reunion

An annual family reunion is one way to replenish the inner strength and Christian bonds that often become forgotten. Family reunions make it possible for members who are separated across the globe to come home. Family members can put aside their routine duties, regroup their thoughts, and begin anew as they celebrate the love of "family."

Whether you you are able to gather for a reunion periodically with your extended family or not, be sure to teach your child the value of corresponding with aunts, uncles, cousins, and grandparents. This helps your child to become rooted in family and gives them a sense of belonging that cannot be taken away.

Take Pride in Your Family's Name

Make a family history book using a photo album and pictures of family members. Enjoy this book with your child and discuss your heritage and roots. This helps your child develop a sense of pride for his family heritage and makes aging an integral part of his young life.

Develop and nurture a relationship with your own parents and grandparents. Phone calls, pictures in the mail, and trips together deepen the caring between a parent and child, no matter what the age. How you treat your parents serves as a role model for how your child will treat you.

Teaching your children family values so they will be able to stand strong when they are tempted requires much time and energy. But as you work at regaining control of your family, you will find that this time was well spent—since moral children who have a special place for family in their hearts will be the result.

Family Time

Sharing meals together is vital as you reclaim the family. As members come together for food and fellowship, affirmation and acceptance are experienced, adding to a child's self-esteem. Use this time to share the following activities with all members.

Discovering Strengths: Ask members to tell their five greatest strengths. Then, ask them to tell two strengths of each member around the table. Take time to share these and enjoy the special gifts in your family. Join hands and close with a simple prayer, thanking God for each person.

Recognizing Gifts: Give each family member a sheet of paper and pencil after dinner. Ask members to write their name at the top of the page, then pass this around the table until they each have someone else's paper. Have members write down the gifts they would be thankful for if they were the person whose name is on the paper. Share these gifts when everyone is through, and talk about the many gifts your family has.

Notes

1. James A. Michener, "What is the Secret of Teaching Values?" *Money* (April 1991), S14.

2. Steve Patterson, "When There's Trouble, Focus on Ethical Values," *Florida Times-Union* (January 10, 1994), B–1.

3. Merton P. Stommen and A. Irene Strommen, *Five Cries of Parents* (New York: Guideposts, 1985), 124.

4. Barbara Kantrowitz, "The Good, The Bad, and The Difference," *Newsweek* (Special Issue, 1991), 48.

5. E. Kent Hayes, "How to Be a Better Parent" *Redbook* (August 1990), 133.

6. Debra Fulghum Bruce, *Making Memories That Count* (Springfield: Chrism, 1994).

7. Joanne Barbara Koch and Linda Nancy Freeman, M.D., *Good Parents for Hard Times* (New York: Fireside,1992), 73.

8. Michael Schulman and Eva Mekler, *Bringing Up a Moral Child* (New York: Addison-Wesley, 1985), 6.

9. Lawrence Kohlberg and Carol Gilligan, "The Adolescent as Philosopher," in *Twelve to Sixteen: Early Adolescence,* ed. Robert Coles et al. (New York: W. W. Norton, 1972).

10. Tracy Johnston, M.A. and Sue Weathington, R.N, "Sex Education for Young Children." *Living Well*: North Florida Edition (Winter 1992).

11. Robin Goldstein, *More Everyday Parenting* (New York: Penguin Books, 1991), 51.

12. *Florida Times-Union,* "Teen Drug Use Climbing," (Febuary 1, 1994), A-1, 9.

13. "First Comes the Baby Carriage," *The Florida Citizen.* (February 1994), 1.

Chapter 5

Take Control of the Time in Your Life

"If only I could move to a new town and make a new start, then I would be happy." "If only I could change jobs, buy a new home, find the right man or woman, get my college degree, have enough to retire on, then I would be happy." "If only I had this. . . . If only I could find that. . . ."

Wait a minute! Aren't we all guilty of looking for happiness in the wrong places? Maybe what we need to do as we work to reclaim our family is to slow down and get in control of the time in our lives . . . then we could feel contentment.

A Louis Harris poll revealed that since 1973 the number of hours Americans say they work actually increased by 20 percent, while the number of leisure hours dropped by 32 percent. We really did not need a poll to tell us that on the average, we all work far too many hours and enjoy it less.

In our family with two working parents and three active teens, we sometimes feel like a ball that someone is bouncing all the time. Up, down . . . down, up. The problem is: When will things ever stop? But the good news is that as you begin to take control of what goes on in your home and reclaim your family, you can stop the bouncing ball. You can take inventory of what is important in your life and redistribute your time to focus on the most meaningful aspects. With some sound and practical steps to regain the time in your life, you can experience inner peace and lifelong happiness.

Stress Zaps Our Time

Someone once said that perhaps stress is just another word for being a parent. Especially with parents who are working too much and enjoying it less, pressure and stress invariably go hand in hand. This stress and feeling out of control are no laughing matter for any of us. Whether it comes from demanding employers, screaming kids, or aggressive drivers during rush hour, stress can sneak up on you and zap all your energy, ruining any creative or quality time you might have wished for. Most of the time you do not even realize you are stressed out . . . until you burn out.

Look at your past week, and mark all the symptoms you have experienced.

How stressed are you?

_____ Stomachache

_____ Headache

_____ Diarrhea

_____ Rapid pulse

_____ Problems with peers at work or family at home

_____ Difficulties at work or at home

_____ Temper tantrums or moodiness

_____ Nightmares or insomnia

_____ Too little sleep

_____ Too much sleep

_____ Complaints from coworkers

_____ Difficulty in concentration
_____ Change in appetite
_____ Nervousness, edginess
_____ Withdrawal
_____ Trembling, sweaty hands
_____ Impatience
_____ Muscle tension
_____ Easy to anger
_____ Loss of interest or enjoyment in life
_____ Chronic fatigue

If you checked more than three boxes, you may be suffering from too much stres. But there is help!

Recognize Warning Signs

Stress actually describes the many demands and pressures that all parents experience to some degree each day. These demands may be physical or emotional in nature, and they require us to change or adapt in some fashion.

Stress can show itself through a wide variety of physical changes and emotional responses and symptoms may vary from one person to the next. Perhaps the most universal sign of stress is a feeling of being pressured or overwhelmed. Other symptoms include:

➤ Physical problems—stomachaches, headaches, diarrhea
➤ Problems getting along with others
➤ Changes in behavior at home—temper outbursts, unexplained anger, or crying for no reason
➤ Regression—behavior that is not age-appropriate
➤ Changes in sleep patterns—nightmares, too little or too much sleep
➤ Communication difficulty— change in personality, such as a withdrawn person requiring much attention or an extrovert becoming withdrawn
➤ Impatience

Worry and tension that are allowed to build up can cause psychological and physical symptoms that can impair your well-being. If you are experiencing a few of these characteristics, your level of stress may be excessive. If left untreated, stress can lead to permanent feelings of helplessness and ineffectiveness.

The leading killers in our society are heart disease, cancer, stroke, diabetes, and atherosclerosis. While researchers look for cures for these diseases, we can eliminate certain risks for getting these diseases; one of the most important risk factors in each category is eliminating stress.

Stress can affect anyone, but busy parents struggling to make ends meet while taking care of active children are particularly vulnerable to this problem. Jesus showed signs of stress when He was in the Garden, and Paul told of circumstances bringing him to the point of despair in 2 Corinthians 1:8, saying "We were really crushed and overwhelmed, and feared we would never live through it" (TLB). While no one is immune to feeling overwhelmed or stressed, we do not have to stay that way.

You can reduce the harmful effect of stress on your life. Realize that stress comes from your response to the pressures. No one can put undue pressure on you unless you accept it, so know what your stress point is—that load in life that you can handle—and eliminate any obligations or pressures that take you over this mark.

Make a list of stresses in your life including obligations and commitments. Some of these responsibilities you must live with—being part of a family, going to work, helping others in the community. Accept those stresses that you cannot solve and learn to live with them, such as illness in the family, a limited budget, or problems with children. But many extra commitments can be eliminated if they overload your system.

Survival Strategies for Decreasing Stress

Try to eliminate stressful situations. When possible, avoid heavy traffic, loud noises, too many people, or making hasty decisions when you feel nervous. Here are some sure-proof methods for responding to stress in appropriate ways:

1. Wake up fifteen minutes earlier on school and work days. We usually wake up earlier than the kids to have some quiet time before the alarms go off. But seeing the tension rise as our teens argued over who was going to shower first made us aware that a new system was needed. Now when our kids are home, each teen rotates a week of the dreaded "early bird" shower. The tension is less, the tempers are not as hot, and school and work mornings are more relaxed. Would early rising and family organization lessen your stress loads on busy mornings?

2. Provide for at least thirty minutes of exercise each day. We have found that when we exercise—bike, walk, run—our moods are much more controlled than if we do not. For our teens, the months they are not participating in swim team, crew, or track are the most stressful months. As we worked to reduce stress, we began to walk daily, and the teens started their own off-season running program. We found that it is hard to be angry or stressed out when you are physically tired.

3. Think before making new commitments. Jesus told of the need to count the cost before taking on anything new (Luke 14:28–33). The biblical passage in Matthew 5:37 instructs us to let our yes be yes and our no be no.

As we work on the stress level in our home, each family member commits to setting reasonable limitations on their time. We each made a comprehensive list of all the things that caused stress, and then vowed to eliminate or avoid those that were not absolutely necessary. For us, this means thinking twice before we volunteer to serve on another committee with evening meetings. For our teenage daughter, this means only tackling one varsity sport per season so she can focus on her studies.

A physician recommended, "When you feel several stress symptoms, erase your weekend. Do nothing but stay home and take care of yourself so you will feel renewed on Monday morning. Then tackle your world one step at a time." Remember when the apostles told Jesus how busy they had been and how tired they were from the pressures?

Jesus affirmed the need for rest by saying, "Come away by yourselves to a lonely place and rest awhile" (Mark 6:31).

Take advantage of that quiet place and spend your time wisely to avoid too much stress.

4. Share the family work load. One of the greatest causes of our stress in our home was constantly being the one with most of the responsibility. When our teens were busy with part-time jobs, babysitting, sports, school, and other activities, good 'ole Mom and Dad were the ones to do the family chores—until we delegated the work between five able bodies. Now each member has one particular area—the bathroom, the den, the kitchen, etc.—and after dinner, twenty minutes is spent straightening up their area before homework or activities can begin.

Remember Jethro advised Moses to share the work load to protect Moses and his people from stress and weariness (Ex. 18:13–27). Sometimes we must share or even eliminate some of our work or stress load in order to avoid feeling trapped.

5. Use destressers when your body signals warn of anxiety. When pressures still mounted, we practiced coping mechanisms with our teens such as breathing deeply, closing eyes and imagining a peaceful scene, or relaxing different body parts intentionally. Deep breathing can fool a stressed-out body and make it think it is relaxed, even when it is not.

Counting to ten before lashing out is another way to gain control. When you are angry, count to ten, walk out of the room, and go for a walk.

6. Make time to be alone with God. In prayer we can turn our problems and worries over to God and realize the inner peace that only He can give. We talked with our teens about making daily time for prayer, writing prayer lists, and checking off answers to prayers as God responded. This has helped all of us to realize that what is stressful today is often forgotten in a few weeks as we learn to let God take control of our lives. We can also eliminate much stress by designating a specific time of the day to think about our "worries"—when we will turn these over to the Lord—and can then replace these with positive thoughts for the rest of the day.

7. Seek help with a support group before you feel over-burdened. Everyone needs someone to talk to—someone who will listen to problems, joys, and concerns. The Bible encourages this support: "Bear one another's burdens, and thus fulfill the law of Christ" (Gal. 6:2). Talk to God, your spouse, your pastor, or your physician. Professional therapists can offer support as well as peers undergoing similar stresses. Often close friends or family members can assist you in stressful times as they listen without giving unsolicited advice. Leaning on your friends, family, or children can be a great asset during these moments.

As you take time to "Be still and know that I am God" (Ps. 46:10, NIV), you will discover a personal relationship with God that can relieve and conquer the most stressful times.

Perfectionism

Are you trying too hard to be a perfect parent and finding that it is adding to an already stress-filled life? Is every detail of every moment fine tuned so that each day is flawless? Do you spend days and nights dwelling on the imperfections of the previous day in order to avoid such mistakes in the future? In short, are you a perfectionist?

Parents who are perfectionists usually cannot handle change or failure in the family. And for those of us who have children, change and failure are experienced daily. Our friend Linda, the mother of an eight and a ten-year-old, told us, "I become so tired and overextended trying to keep up with my kids that it shows up in my personality by the end of the week. I want everything that they do to go perfectly, including school behavior, grades, and how they act at home. The problem is that I don't have a very Christian attitude toward my own children sometimes when something goes wrong."

Other parents who try too hard to be perfect become their own best critics. "I begin to feel like a failure if my attempts at dealing with my two sons aren't perfect by my high standards," Sam, the father of eleven-year-old twin boys said. "I reprimand myself in hopes I will deal better with their behavior and conflicts. But I become so moody and angry inside no one can stand to be around me."

If you are like Sam and Linda, you want everything— well—perfect. You not only strive for excellence in all you attempt, you also seek perfection in everything for which you feel responsible. Always struggling to achieve the best in whatever you do, you feel driven to get ahead no matter what. While your calling to Christian discipleship does demand that you do your best, a constant push for perfection can cause undue stress in the lives of each member of your family— which results in hazards to everyone's mental and physical well-being.

Look at the following statements and questions, and check all that apply. How do you rate as the perfect parent?

_____ 1. I expect perfection in my expectations of myself and my children at home, at school, at church, and at play?

_____ 2. If I make a mistake in parenting, my children will think I am a failure.

_____ 3. Getting out of control while dealing with my child's problem upsets me.

_____ 4. If I push my children hard enough to succeed at school and activities, their lives will go perfectly.

_____ 5. I feel embarrassed if my children mess up at school or in public with their decisions or grades.

_____ 6. I'm less of a person if I can't get my child to obey me 100 percent of the time.

_____ 7. If my children don't use their time wisely, I'm a failure at motivating them.

_____ 8. I have dreams of giving up sometimes because of the pressure I create for myself.

_____ 9. I'm unsatisfied with myself if I feel my child is only average in his successes.

_____ 10. If my child makes even the smallest mistake, I scold him immediately and then feel miserable.

_____ 11. I sometimes push my child to do more than he or I can tolerate with activities to "enrich him."

_____ 12. I feel jealous if my friend's child gets an honor or award and my child does not receive this.

If you checked more than three or four of these questions, it is time to reevaluate your motivation for being a parent and set some new priorities.

Recognize the Problem

A stumbling block in parenting is to have unrealistic expectations of yourself. These expectations can become self-defeating because your children, who are often out of your control, obstruct your perfection.

Trying to be "Super Mom" or "Wonder Dad" may become a form of earning your way into God's favor. But in doing so you may block the grace of God in your life. Perfectionism can be a burden when you do not allow yourself and your adventurous child the risky necessity of making mistakes, for mistakes are often the key to growth and development. In our family, our greatest moments of personal growth and bonding occurred not during a perfect day, but when someone messed up or failed. Oh, how our Lord brought us together during those tense moments!

See Perfectionism Through Faith

The Bible recognizes perfectionism as an issue for Christians. Jesus commanded us to be perfect, and Paul recognized our imperfection: "For our knowledge is imperfect and our prophecy is imperfect; but when the perfect comes, the imperfect will pass away" (1 Cor. 13:9–10, RSV). In Philippians 3:7–14, Paul said that he was not already perfect, but that he was pressing on to become something more. Christians are to rate their ability with sober judgment, each according to the degree of faith apportioned by God to them (Rom. 12:3–8).

As a human being you are imperfect, and yet as a person of faith, you are pressing on to become something more than you are now. Knowing this tension, you can make some changes in your expectation of yourself. These changes can help you relax so that you can enjoy God's grace at work in you to bring you to wholeness and well-being.

Ways to Cope with Perfectionism

Set goals and priorities. First, before we can enjoy parenting with its many joys and stumbling blocks, we must get our priorities straight in our personal lives. If you are overcommitted in other areas, initiate a plan to restructure where you spend your time.

Setting priorities requires you to make firm decisions about what you want to achieve today, this week, and your lifetime. In our busy lives, we always revamp priorities by making lists. Write down all of the activities, organizations, and commitments to which you devote yourself. Be sure to include tasks that you must do, as well as activities that you do for your own pleasure. When the list is complete, mark these commitments A, B, and C, depending on their importance (A being utmost important and C being the least important).

Of course, our first priority should be God. If you are too busy to heed God's voice, then you are too busy! If you are too busy to perform some service in His kingdom, then you are too busy. We must not forget that there will come a time when our relationship with Him will be the only priority that will matter. Family responsibilities should come next on your list, but you should also make time for personal hobbies and interests that are yours. Place a reasonable limit on the number and variety of commitments that you make, and post this on your refrigerator to remind you of your commitments.

Set attainable goals. Set attainable goals for each area on your list, and make sure you consider the time involved to attain each of these goals. Do not confuse daily, short-term, and long-term goals. When you set attainable goals, you ensure that the goals will be within your reach. Perfectionists usually reach for goals that are too difficult. Then, when faced with failure, they feel personal humiliation.

"When my boss was hospitalized last month with heart problems, I assured him that I would take over until he returned," said Steven, a father of a seven-year-old daughter. "But I was also coaching Melody's T-ball team, teaching Sunday School at church, and taking night courses. I was so distraught in wanting every avenue of my life to go smoothly that nothing went smoothly! And my relationship with my wife and Melody suffered the most."

Know your limits and be realistic. As you get your priorities straight and learn that it is okay to relax, start to be realistic with your limitations. It is much easier to say no to a persuasive friend when you have thought out the situation beforehand. Review your calendar frequently, and weigh the alternatives of making new commitments. Talk to your family members about their needs. Would another commitment stretch you too thin? Would your personal time be eliminated? Take a firm stand and if you are confronted with a new obligation that makes you overcommitted, say no and mean it. You will be respected in the long run for your honesty.

Learn how to say "no." Saying "no" takes practice. Being honest when saying "no" is often difficult, especially for enthusiastic Christians. If you are too honest, people will accuse you of being blunt and inconsiderate. "Don't you care about our class (or group or cause)?" they ask. But, if you hide your feelings and overcommit yourself to every person who asks for your involvement, you resent the activity and, this resentment will show. Your participation will begin to reflect a phony and insincere attitude.

Being able to say "no" depends partly on how you feel about yourself. Do you like yourself? Assertiveness psychology, a new approach to building and maintaining self-respect, says the more you stand up for yourself and act in a manner you respect, the more you will be comfortable with yourself. By exercising basic rights of being a person, you can change your attitudes and feelings about yourself.[1] And choosing your involvement in life is your basic right as a child of God.

Consider several polite ways you could say "no" to a friend or community leader. Write them down and practice saying them. For example:

➤ "No, I have other plans that day."
➤ "No, I don't feel comfortable leading that study."
➤ "Yes, I do enjoy singing, but I can't commit to the choir while my children are still so young."

➤ "That is Pete's only day off, and we like to spend it as a family. I won't be able to do the typing."

➤ "I don't enjoy leading arts and crafts. I'm sorry. Perhaps I could take the roll for the class."

➤ "Friday is the only night I have with the wife and kids. Sorry!"

➤ "I'm going to be a member and watch how the meetings are run this year. Maybe in a few years I will take a leadership role."

➤ "Coach the T-ball team? I need to spend more time this year watching so I can learn the game."

As you practice saying "no," avoid leading the person on with an added phrase such as "Maybe tomorrow I will do it" unless you really intend to follow through. If you mean "no," say "no."

Remain tactful when saying no. Tact is that delicate perception of knowing the right thing to say or do without offending the other person. When you use tact in saying no, you must be sensitive to the person asking the question. Instead of downplaying the activity or commitment as being unimportant, simply refuse politely. Rather than making the person feel rejected, explain that you are overcommitted at the moment. There are many ways you can interject tact in your conversation that can lead to a positive outcome without your bearing the burden of overinvolvement.

When you make commitments, stick with them. As you evaluate the time in your life, be sure to carefully meet the commitments you have already made. For some people making commitments is very difficult. According to one pastor, children in America today have learned fear of commitment from adults, especially their parents. "Children watch their parents hesitate in making decisions everyday of their life with fear as the motivating factor," Ron said. "Perhaps the adult is afraid of making the wrong decision which could cause undue embarrassment or unhappiness."

"Making the wrong choice such as in a career or financial investment could result in fear or rejection by family and loved ones. Some adults are afraid to launch out in making a firm choice for fear of failure. If you have depended on others to make decisions all your life, fear of becoming independent creates alarming thoughts."

At a recent parenting workshop, the leader noted that one of the gravest problems in America today was in the home. He said, "Spouses hold up the popular choice of separation or divorce if they ever sense disillusionment or dissatisfaction. And this instability leads to lack of commitment from children. America's children are learning how to be experts in the options game as weak parents allow them to choose activities that produce the most immediate pleasure when faced with making responsible decisions."

Playing the options game is dangerous for Christians, but the biggest hazard is seen in the home. Family units break down as strength diminishes and as parents walk a tightrope in their relationships. Morals and values become weak and waiver if no firm stand is taken; children are unsure of what is right or wrong.

Jesus' ministry was one of making choices. As He confronted people in different situations, He encouraged them to make firm commitments and decisions about their lives—to choose between good and evil. The uniqueness of the New Testament lies in this new freedom that Jesus taught, breaking away from the bondage of the Old Testament law.

As Christians, God calls us to be obedient in the midst of having freedom. This summons involves our taking responsibility to act. By taking action and making firm commitments, we will model security and responsibility to our developing children.[2]

Yes, It's OK to Be Average

Allow yourself the privilege of being average in some areas of your life. Yes, it is okay to relax sometimes! Athletes excel in only one or two sports because of the special development of the muscles required for each sport. Great golfers are usually lousy football players. Good writers may not know how to bake a layer cake. Similarly, you do not have to be the perfect parent in all avenues of raising children. In our home, Bob enjoys doing the sports teams with the kids; he has coached soccer, baseball, softball, and swim teams in the past years. On the other hand, Deb does not enjoy sports, and she does not even pretend to understand how to play. But in the evening hours, the children always come to her for consultation, problem solving, and suggestions for class projects. As parents who are not perfect, we have found that it is really okay to be average at some things in your life. Build on your positive points with your children and feel good about this.

Work with Others

In Romans 12:6, Paul says, "Having gifts that differ according to the grace given to us, let us use them" (RSV). You need to rely on others and their gifts as well as on yourself and your gifts. Use your special talents, and rejoice in the gifts and endurance God is giving you. But recognize and accept your limitations and the need to allow others to exercise their gifts.

Caroline, another close friend, adores music and sang in the choir at our church. When the choir director resigned last year, Caroline enthusiastically accepted the assignment of organizing and directing the children's choir so her three daughters would have a musical experience.

"I know nothing of directing," she cried after a frustrating rehearsal. "Here I am, trying to count beats, read notes, and teach lyrics at the same time. I feel so inadequate. Yet I feel like I should be able to do this." This past spring as reorganization for the choir program began, Caroline chose to volunteer as a choir mom and assisted the new choir director instead of leading the children in singing.

Realize what strengths you do have, and use these to the best advantage as you parent your children. Understand your limitations, and work with them as best you can within your Christian home.

Grow Through Failure

You have to learn that it is all right to fail. But failure can lead to disappointment and depression if not handled in a positive way. Learn to interpret a failure not as a personal rejection, but as an opportunity to grow.

Once you learn to risk failure and disappointment, you can begin to move forward in your life. Many stories from the Bible teach us how others dealt with personal tragedies and rose above them. For example, Job's struggles with living give us insight into suffering and how faith in God can sustain us. During times of failure and disappointment, God offers us comforting assurance, loving forgiveness, and tremendous strength.

Learn to Laugh

As you accept your imperfection, learn to laugh at yourself, yes, even at your parenting skills. There is probably nothing more difficult than to take yourself lightly, but in order to break the perfectionist habit, you will need to stop taking every mistake so seriously.

Lucinda, a single parent told about working full-time when her daughter was a preschooler:

> After getting up at 5 A.M. to make breakfasts, bag lunches, do the laundry, and get Allison to preschool before work, I can hardly make it to crawl in bed at night.

Allison, who napped all afternoon at day-care, was always full of energy during the evening. I knew that reading stories to her was important, but I had to do what was right for both of us. One Saturday, I tape-recorded her favorite stories and nursery rhymes, and even played some music on the tape. I closed the tape with some prayers and simple Scripture verses. Now at 8:00 P.M. each night, I read Allison her bedtime story and we say our prayers, then as she starts to beg for more and more stories, I turn the tape on beside her bed. She listens contently and drifts to sleep; I get to crawl in bed with a smile on my face and not feel guilty about ignoring her.

Be at Peace with God

God can fill any inadequacies or insecurities you feel in your life, so learn to be at peace with God. His grace forgives you and frees you to live with your imperfection. God's love will strengthen you to move toward perfection. Through daily prayer, Bible study, and fellowship with other Christians, you are constantly reminded of God's presence and can know yourself to be loved for who you are, not for what you do or how well you do it.

There is no time in anyone's life to be a perfect parent. If you are, why not make plans now to slow down, get your personal life in order, and let yourself make some mistakes. Remember the song "Jesus loves me, this I know, for the Bible tells me so." Radiating this love to your children is the Christian parent's primary goal, for life is too short and too precious to spend it trying to be perfect.

To review, we can take steps to get our perfectionism under control. Here are the basic principles:

➤ Reevaluate your priorities.
➤ Reassess the commitments you have already made.
➤ Make firm decisions and stick with these.

➤ Take responsibility for your decisions.
➤ Understand that there are things in your life that you have control over and things that you do not.
➤ Determine the important factors of your life, and set your own limits.

Get in Control of Homework Time

All kids need help in getting organized and making study plans. Our three children needed some instructions to help them learn to manage homework time and reduce their stress. Some of what we learned may help in your family.

Set Aside Time Each School Night

This could be a one to two-hour period, depending on your child's needs. If home study hall is from 7:00 to 9:00 P.M., the child is responsible for organizing his or her other activities around this. If there is no assigned homework, the child can find books to read or work on another school project that may be due later.

Set the Tone for Study

Have a certain place for your child to study so he or she understands "same time, same place." This can be in the bedroom with a desk or at the dining room table. While some children are distracted with background noises, studies do show that classical music may enable child to learn even more if played softly. Make sure that the telephone is off-limits except for brief "homework discussions," and the television should be turned off.

Provide supplies that your child will need ahead of time, including a calendar, pencils, pens, sharpener, paper, notebooks, dictionary, ruler, and calculator. Check with the classroom teachers for a list of other study tools.

Set Study Goals

On a blank sheet of paper, have your child write a list of goals each evening, including homework assignments, review lists, studying for tests, rewriting notes, and recommended reading. The child can designate a certain amount of time for each project, then check this off after it is completed. By breaking up the two-hour period into small sections, the child can focus on the task at hand, take a snack break or walk around, then go back to more homework.

Sample Two-Hour Study Time

Homework Goals	Time:
Review Spanish vocabulary words	15 min.
Read Social Studies and work on map	30 min.
Take snack break	15 min.
Do Math homework and organize notebook	30 min.
Finish essay for English	15 min.
Study for Health test	15 min.

Set the Example

Children are not born knowing how to study. With firm parental direction and a positive attitude, your child will know that homework is important and is his or her responsibility. Use this quiet time in the evenings to catch up on your reading, pay bills, or write letters so your home environment complements good study habits.

Slowing Down the Hurried Child

As you become more aware of time management in your family and gain precious moments that used to be filled with empty activities, evaluate your child's afterschool and weekend schedule. Many children are so over-scheduled that they are missing out on childhood. Some parents fill each afternoon with organized sports, dance lessons, music lessons, scouting, church activities—all so the child does not become "bored."

Make sure your child has ample time during the week to be free—to create, play quietly, think, experience, daydream, watch clouds, and be bored—yes, bored! When children are bored, they are forced to look inside themselves and come up with great ideas to overcome this suffering. Many great inventions, musical compositions, and books were created not when someone was too stimulated and entertained by others, but rather when the person was quiet, pensive, and possibly bored.

Parents must control their child's schedule so that meaningful commitments are made and "free" time is also included for self-discovery.

Part-time Parenting

Find Time for the Working Parent

When a close friend went through a divorce last year, she was forced into the working world. Her most difficult problem was not adjusting to her nine-to-five job, but rather frustration with the guilt of being a working parent.

"I am a weekend parent," Sue said to us honestly. "I have no time to spend with my daughters except on the weekend. I enjoy this time, but I've run out of ways to entertain them. I am sick of nature movies, the zoo, the park, and fast food restaurants. What more can I do?"

Parenting in the nineties has become a real problem for most families. For single parents like Sue, a lifestyle has been rearranged; she must now change her priorities to include a demanding career along with raising her family. Other parents who have experienced having to go back to the job force after being at home with the children know about the guilt of part-time parenting and not spending as much time at home as you want to.

"I feel like a Santa Claus trying to win my child's affection," one single father said. "After awhile, being on-the-go constantly on the weekend to make up for absences during the week takes its toll on everyone."

Many working parents who travel or who are away from the home at odd hours are also confronted with the guilt of being a part-time parent. Sharon, a newspaper reporter and mother of twin girls, runs a freelance typing business in her home. She is called out of town on assignments frequently and must leave the girls with her husband. "Even though I am home most of the time," she said, "I often don't have time to be a real mom until the weekend. I try so hard to prove my love to them that sometimes I can't wait until Monday morning comes to get back to work."

Parents who combine dual careers with raising children experience many hazards as they try to overdo on the weekend. Many parents spend Saturdays with their young at the movies, shopping for the latest toys, or eating fast foods at popular restaurants. And while these outings may prove fun for the moment, they can leave both the parent and the child feeling empty and alone. Trying to fill every weekend with constant entertainment can give children an idea that life is a plush, fantasy world.

Another hazard families may experience if the parent is trying to play the role of "Super Mom" or "Super Dad" on the weekend is that children will lack a true role-model. If your only interaction as the parent is sitting side-by-side while being entertained, the children will not know how you cope in genuine life situations. How can they contend with frustration if the parents never face it on the weekends? How can the children deal with conflict, sorrow, or rejection if all they see is their parent ready for celebrations? Children learn coping mechanisms for life as they observe a caring parent in action—dealing with a personal problem, facing tragedy or disappointment, or managing stress and anxiety in a positive manner.

A probable hazard in overindulging children as a part-time parent is that somewhere, someday, you will resent the time, money, and energies you spent in creating this false environment. We have struggled with the tendency to over-buy "treats" for our children after a busy work week. While these treats or rewards may be inexpensive, we get angry at our inability to control guilty impulses and work at spending quality time with our children instead of money.

When you intentionally provide your child with gifts and constant entertainment to make up for lost time, you are not doing so in the child's best interest. You may be creating a phony environment of fun and games to relieve your own guilt. A close friend admitted, "When I went back to work to help put our son in college, I felt so much guilt leaving eight-year-old Micah with a sitter after school. Every day I brought her a candy bar; it was my way of saying "I'm sorry," I suppose. Anyway, one day I was hurrying and forgot her treat. Micah was furious. She rejected me the entire evening simply because I had conditioned her to accept me only with the candy. I sure learned a lesson."

If you are a working parent and feel this conflict and guilt, you can provide a balanced situation at home that includes a regular routine, work and play, and even some conflict.

Your Children Are Not Special Guests

The first step involves realizing that your children are not special guests that you must entertain and reward. Children should see you in a relaxed atmosphere where you can be a close family. Shawn, a preteen, spoke of his divorced father, "Everytime I go to see Dad, he is having a good time. Sure it is fun to go boating each weekend, but I wonder how Dad really feels since he left. We haven't talked since the divorce."

Often parents give the children constant fun and ignore the warmth and companionship that goes along with this. Entertainment can have its place on the weekend, along with staying at home, sharing household responsibilities, and interacting as a family.

Keep Your Routine on Weekends

You can relieve your guilt by keeping a normal routine each weekend. If you are a single parent and wash your car on the weekends when the kids are not with you, get them to help you on the weekends you see them. Other activities might include cleaning the garage, watching a baseball game on TV, or working on a joint hobby

Instead of following the pattern that children must eat out while with you on the weekends, let them help you prepare the meals. Children can learn cooperation and responsibility as they help you fix the food. And you can be more relaxed in a home environment as you partake of the meal you all work to prepare.

Use the Weekend to Get Personal

Quality time is important when you are a part-time parent. And when your parenting attention is limited to weekends, you must make use of every minute to talk with your children and to really listen. Ask about their school activities, their peers, their personal feelings, their dreams. Try to read between the lines as you develop a close relationship during this time.

As you see your children in a relaxed home environment, they can start to feel secure in being themselves. You can feel comfortable in knowing that you do not have to put on a "super parent" act for them and in knowing that your part-time parenting is genuine, filled with love, and guilt-free.

Family Memories

"Every Saturday morning is Dad's day to wait on the family as he cooks breakfast for everyone," Julia shared. "My husband designs his own menu the week before, and the kids can't wait to see what new surprises he makes for us."

"One morning we had a cereal and fresh fruit picnic outside, then another cold, winter Saturday, we enjoyed hot chocolate and homemade cinnamon buns by the fire. This is a memory our children will have forever."

Ron, a parent of three children, said: "The Christmas memories we are forming for our children are very special. For the past twelve years on Christmas morning, I have taken movies of the children as they open their presents. I start the video by saying, 'Kids, this is the BEST Christmas ever!' and the children respond by saying the same thing. Sure, it's a bit corny now as they are older, but it is a memory they'll never forget!"

Another family we know reserves Sunday dinner as being special in their home. "Each member takes his or her turn in planning the meal, buying the foods, and preparing this in a creative manner," Sheila said. "We've had all sorts of concoctions from meatless spaghetti to chicken lasagna to oven-roasted vegetables. But the pride and joy each member feels is wonderful. It's our 'family thing.'"

The Wilson family exercises together each evening. While the parents ride bicycles, one toddler sits behind John on his bike, and eight-year-old Trina rides her bike alongside Marnie. "We stay in shape and have a good time—together," John said. "It's something the kids will remember."

One Georgia family started a "Family Round Robin" tradition as they wrote a lengthy letter to relatives who lived in California. The West Coast family, in turn, added to the letter and sent it on to another sister living in Missouri, who added more pages and sent the entire message to the grandparents who lived in Washington, D.C. By the time the initial family received the letter back, it had traveled across the United States and was nine pages filled with informative and humorous family stories. This tradition continues every three months and is enjoyed by all.

The Myers family in Florida has cookouts every Saturday night. "Even when it rains, we cook out," Bob said. "It is something that the kids look forward to and count on each week. And it is time we know we'll spend together."

How Will They Remember You?

After all is said and done in your family, can you say that your time was well-spent? In other words, have you made time to build long-lasting relationships with your children so that important memories result?

The question is important, because memories are powerful forces in shaping our lives—they are nothing consider lightly. Our memories are a lot like sinkholes or volcanoes. On the surface there is the obvious hole in the ground; you can see it and measure it. But these surface features are only the beginning; in fact, the surface is merely the by-product of what's going on deep down inside.

Memory has two levels. The surface level of memory is the memory of a certain room in a certain house on a certain street; the memory of the smell of a particular perfume; the memory of the aroma of baking; the memory of hands worn rough by years of labor. Though important, these are only on the surface. Another level of memory is that deep inner reservoir of memory called the subconscious, out of which comes the motivation and power of our lives. From our subconscious comes our actions, which come out of our values.

The writer of Proverbs spoke about the power of the subconscious: "Keep your heart with all vigilance; for from it flow the springs of life" (Prov. 4:23, RSV). Jesus said that out of the heart come those things which either make or destroy a person (Luke 6:45, RSV). Both of these statements caution us to be careful what you feed into your memory, since it will eventually become the motivating force of your life.

So, think about it. Years from now, will your children, your greatest investment, have wonderful memories of the times they spent with you?

An important task of parenting is shaping memories. Parents can intentionally choose for their children the kinds of experiences that will help them develop good values to guide them toward acting wholesomely and responsibly in adulthood.

We have asked ourselves the same question. What will our children say about us? First, we hope our three children will say that we truly loved and respected them. Psychologists tell us that the single piece of personality equipment which a child acquires is his self-concept. And the most important thing we can do to help children develop a healthy self-concept is to let them know that we love and respect them— that they are real people to us.

A year ago Deb arrived early at our daughter's Sunday School class, where she was going to volunteer as an assistant. Jason came into the room with his grandmother. "Good morning," Deb said in greeting to the pair. The grandmother nudged Jason. "Say good morning, dear."

Jason just stood with a timid look on his face, so Deb tried to engage him in conversation. "Would you like to help me pass out some papers?" she asked. Again his grandmother responded for him. "Oh, yes. Of course he would. Jason is very helpful at home."

Jason took the papers without a word. "Jason," Deb asked as she looked directly at him, "did you bring any offering for the mission basket?" And one more time, Grandmother interrupted his thoughts by stating, "Oh, no. I forgot to give him any today." But as she was talking, Jason's face lit up and he spoke. "I did bring some money!" He reached into his pocket and put three shiny pennies in the basket. Then he looked up at his grandmother and said, "See, Grandmommy. My teacher thinks I'm real."

May our children know that we think they are real!

Second, we hope our children will say that we loved this world and cared for it. We do believe that this is God's world, and we are responsible for it. We want our children to know that it matters to us what kind of world we pass on to them. And we want to invest ourselves in this world as part of the solution, instead of as a part of the problem. We want our children to see us as persons who conserved energy, cared for the environment, and took pride in our home. As we take time to recycle newspapers, turn off unused lights in our home, and pick up trash at our church playground, may our children learn from our example and continue this practice in their adult lives.

Third, we hope our children say we were fun to be with. We enjoy letting our "parent" guard down once in a while. While our home is structured for discipline, it is also a place for celebration and fellowship. Songs and laughter are common in our home and help our family members to feel good about being alive.

We hope that our children will see us live the Christian life throughout the week, not just during worship on Sunday morning. As we live the life set by the example of Christ, may our children see that it is a life of joy, promise, and celebration. We pray that our children will be able to say, "Being a Christian was the most exciting thing I ever saw my mom and dad do!" We hope that this sound of laughter and joy will never be absent from our home.

Fourth, and most important, our greatest and highest hope is that our children will be able to say, "My parents loved God and lived their lives as disciples of Jesus Christ."

Do you remember how Paul found Christ? He was traveling along the Damascus Road when suddenly there was lightning and thunder. He fell to the ground, struck blind by the presence of God; he had to be literally torn out of his past.

That is how it was for Paul, but not for Timothy. In fact, Paul did not tell Timothy he had to be struck blind by lightning. He simply said, "I am reminded of your sincere faith, a faith that dwelt first in your grandmother Lois and your mother Eunice and now, I am sure, dwells in you. Hence, I remind you to rekindle the gift of God that is within you" (2 Tim. 1:5–6, RSV).

Somehow the Spirit of God dipped into Timothy's subconscious, grabbed hold of the embers of faith that had been planted there by his grandmother and his mother, and set them aflame so that Timothy became a great follower of Christ.

In the home, often the parent is the only example of Christianity a child experiences. Often, the only prayer a child hears is the parent's. When children rebel at home, the Christian faith may not seem to hold much meaning for them at the time. Yet even if those seeds of faith you planted seem to be lying dormant, they will eventually germinate and come to maturity.

May we plant those same seeds in our children's lives, so that someday the Spirit may be able to touch them and bring them to a personal commitment to Jesus Christ. May the prayer we offer every evening as a family glow warmly in their memory as they mature and move on to independent Christian adulthood. If we are the only examples of Christians our children know, then may we stand firmly in the convictions we believe in each day of our life. What will they say about us—about you?

If "it only takes a spark to get a fire going," we pray that the spark of Christian living is alive and well in the memory of our children.

Family Time

1. Pick one night a week to be family night. Let a different member each week plan the menu or activity, and do not let other plans interrupt this special evening.

2. Make the luncheon meal after church on Sunday a special family dinner. Cooking ahead and setting the table the night before can ease the crunch many busy families feel in sticking with a tradition like this.

3. At your regular evening meal, go around the table before the prayer and let each person tell one interesting or happy moment about the day. Do not let mealtime be a place for arguments or depressing conversation.

4. After dinner and before homework begins, spend ten to fifteen minutes just laughing with your children. This could be telling jokes, singing songs, or listening to funny stories that happened during the day.

5. If you have teenagers who want to go out with friends on the weekend, let family night be Thursday evening. This could be a special dinner or even going out to a restaurant. The important fact is that you are all together—a family.

6. Develop family traditions that are "just for you." This may be a certain dessert that is served during the holidays, adding a Christmas ornament to the tree that represents each family member, or writing a family letter that is sent to love ones periodically. Find that certain tradition that you can call your own, and let your children feel pride in this.

7. Sit together in church each week. Let this be that special time where hearts are cleansed and open to God's love and to the love of other family members.

8. Choose names at the beginning of each week and don't let anyone know who you picked. Encourage family members to pray for that person and to do something special—make their bed, put a special note at the table for them, or put a treat under their pillow—without letting them know. This

gives members a feeling of expectation that something good will happen that week.

9. Pray together as a family each day. We gather to pray at the dinner table. You might choose to do this at breakfast, before school, or before you put the children to bed. Let your family members know that prayer is important in your home.

10. During the holiday season, ask your pastor for the name of a needy family and practice benevolence. Go shopping with your children and choose food items and gifts for this family. Let your children experience the joy of giving as you tell them the importance of taking care of all God's children.

11. Adopt a patient at a local nursing home. You might take gifts periodically, write notes, or sing Christmas carols during the holiday season.

12. Hold family devotions each night (see chapter 1 for more ideas on family devotions). Gather devotional material and print suggested Bible verses on index cards for each member to use in daily prayer time. During these devotions together as a family, let members share their feelings and experiences of the day and how Christ has touched their lives.

13. Do not let the years get away from you! Remember that your two-year-old will never be a toddler again. There will never be another third grade play or middle school band concert. Make time each day to talk and interact with your children. Celebrate their activities and encourage their dreams. Tell them you love them and laugh with them, for the time you spend now will be a memory in years to come.

Notes

[1]James Allen Sparks, *Potshots at the Preacher* (Nashville: Abingdon, 1979), 79.

[2]Debra Fulghum Bruce, *Making Memories That Count* (Springfield: Chrism, 1994), 130.

Chapter 6

Take Control of Your Family Income

What has happened to the family in the past three decades? In a nation where family stability was once the rule, we have become a people out of control. Take Ellie, for example. "If only we had $300 dollars more each month," she decided, "I know that we could make ends meet." A few weeks later they did receive this extra income, but did it make a difference?

Ellie (not her real name), a thirty-seven-year-old dental hygienist and mother of three young children, works long nine-hour days with her dentist-husband to keep their high standard of living. "Where did that extra money go?" Ellie complained. "I tried to save some for our tithe, but there were just so many other bills, and I had promised the twins they could start karate lessons. Our savings is gone, and we never have any extra money. Will we ever get in control?"

Ben admits to feeling the same way—out of control in his life. "It all started when our teenager daughter had to have a car like the other young people at school," he told us. "So we took money out of her college fund and bought her a used one. The insurance bills for a teenage driver were unbelievable, then she had an accident one rainy night—her fault. I'm now working a part-time job at night—just to pay for Miranda's car. When will the treadmill end?"

Samuel and Anita are another one example of how families lose control of their finances. "After graduating from college, we got married and immediately started a small bookstore together," Anita said. "We were so excited about this joint venture! I took care of the bookkeeping, while Samuel waited on customers. Things were tight right from the beginning; we had no capital because everything was invested in the shop. Then the bills started coming in—college loans for both of us, car payments, insurance premiums, the rent on the house. It was overwhelming."

"If that wasn't enough, Anita got pregnant," Samuel said. "We hadn't planned for this and had no health insurance. We almost got evicted from our house once because we were three months behind in our rent, and then Anita had to go to bed for several months because of problems with the pregnancy. We finally declared bankruptcy and took day jobs to pay off some of the bills. Maybe someday we will see our dream of owning our business, but for the next ten years, we will be working just to get out of debt."

We Need Help!

Have we all not felt that way? Is working to get out of debt your motivation for work? In our family we have wished for a little more money to add to our already stretched budget or hoped for more time in our too-busy day; we all want to take control of our family and of our life. But how do we begin?

This chapter is for those families who are out of control with their finances and budget. Millions of families are living from paycheck to paycheck every week simply because they have made the wrong financial choices. It doesn't have to be this way! We have learned how to reclaim the family budget. In this chapter there are charts, schedules, lists, and tips so you can start today and evaluate where your income is going, then make plans to get in control with your revenue, bills, and spending.

As you read this chapter, know that you can make a difference in your family's financial security. Give thanks to God for your many blessings, and ask Him to lead you through any family monetary crisis that you might have. Read all the financial material possible so you can understand how to spend your money wisely. Subscribe to magazines and obtain books to help you prepare and implement a sound financial plan for your family.

Perhaps you have been affected by the most serious downsizing of corporate America in our history. In recent years tens of thousands of workers throughout our nation, blue collar and white collar, have been laid off. Armed services, federal, state, and city budgets have been drastically reduced, creating even more job losses. Those affected have seen their careers severely disrupted, cars and homes repossessed, and their savings diminished. The good news is that the worst may be over, and families are now fighting back; the American spirit is alive and you can get in control once again.

We have discovered that getting in control of your income and expenses is most important to achieve the inner peace and security that we strive for in our homes. Society constantly tempts us to lose control and "keep up with the Joneses." In one day, think of all the propaganda you and your children hear from television and radio. Advertisers constantly remind us that we will be so much happier and more successful if we have the proper label on our dresses and suits, a luxury car, basketball shoes, a wide-screen television, a voice-activated VCR, the latest video camera, the ultimate stereo system, a health club membership, our own tanning salon, a time-share membership, more credit cards, and on. The problem is this: If we have all these "things," then why are we not happy?

Let's look at how we can stop this vicious cycle of too many bills and not enough income, and finally get in control of family finances with God's help.

In this chapter on family finance, we will point you in the right direction. But it will take a strong commitment from your family members to gain control of the finances. Controlling your family's finances is just like the economy, the stock market, or operating a business. There will be ups and downs, good times and bad times. How you respond to these fluctuations will determine the ultimate stability of your family's finances.

Take Responsibility for Your Money

The first step in gaining control of your finances begins with a personal relationship with God as you learn what the Bible says about finances. A topical Bible will guide you to passages on family money, debt, taxes, work, and savings, but the basic principle of family finances is found in the Gospel of John: "Ask, and you will receive" (John 16:24). Now, contrary to what some people believe, this Scripture does not mean that whatever we ask for God will automatically provide. Rather, this spiritual promise for believers has two basic meanings: God will give inner peace and provide for our worldly needs. God does not promise material riches or our "wants," but His Word can guide us to make the right decisions for our family in the secular world of finances.

Remember that one-tenth of our income does not belong to us at all! The Bible tells us that this percentage is "God's tithe." The tithe is the first check that should be written each time you pay bills. We use the system of "pay God, pay yourself, then pay others." This will assure you of meeting your Christian obligation, having substantial savings, and paying your creditors what is owed.

You Will Be Tempted

Most people have unlimited desires but limited resources. After all, the syndrome of keeping up with the Joneses can push your family to the breaking point. The control of these desires—which results from knowing that God will provide for your needs—will guide your family to financial security. Of course, we mean financial security, not unlimited wealth or a get-rich-quick scheme. This chapter will discuss developing earthly financial security as you lean on your spiritual security.

Beware of False Prophets

As we are warned of false prophets in our spiritual life, in our financial life profits and promises of wealth can be found everywhere—on television commercials and programs, in lectures, in books and tapes, and even from the pulpit as promoters guarantee material profit based on the size of your monetary giving and not on your basic faith.

The Christian Work Ethic Will Prevail

From early on in their marriage, our friends Tom and Katherine have had deep religious convictions and meaningful priorities. As the parents of two teens, they have applied Christian faith and action to every family involvement. They have tithed 10 percent of their family income, saved money from each paycheck, and been involved in all areas of their church.

"We built our home on a Christian foundation, carefully followed a budget, and controlled our purchases, and we paid cash instead of the excessive interest on credit cards and installment purchases," Tom said. "It has not been easy. We have done without when other families were going into debt to make luxury purchases. Sometimes that was hard to explain to our daughters 'why' we didn't live in the largest home or drive the latest automobile or take lengthy vacations. But we are also living proof that families can be in control on their finances and live stress-free and debt-free."

This couple bought late model used cars instead of new and drove them for as long as they could. Katherine belonged to wholesale clubs, only bought items on sale at department stores, and shopped garage sales for used furniture and clothing for the children. With their two teens near college age, they are not concerned about the skyrocketing costs of higher education. "We started a college fund when the girls were small and have added to this regularly," Tom said. "Now they both have enough money in their funds to pay for half their college education. The other half will be funded by the girls—student loans, work studies, scholarships and grants, and summer job savings. It will help them appreciate their education and be more responsible in college."

There are millions of families like this one in America today; families who have not fallen into the financial trap of "keeping up with the Joneses" and who have been able to live well on their income, whatever it may be. As you continue to read this chapter, you will see how your family can also be successful in gaining control of your finances.

Gain Control of Your Family's Income

Open communication with all family members on a regular basis will reinforce the overall plans. At family meetings and in conversation, talk with your children and listen to their responses to create a lifestyle that will best suit your needs. Areas of discussion will include housing, cars, savings, investments, life insurance, church tithe, allowances, budget, credit cards, wills, and the designated bookkeeper. From these discussions you can move into the family budget and plan with anticipation. Rather than looking at the budget as a restriction on spending in the negative sense, you can look at it as a road map to achieve your goals as outlined.

If making out a budget is your idea of torture, be patient. The families that get control of their finances believe that a carefully thought-out budget cannot only reduce expenses and increase financial security but can actually be fun as short- and long-term goals are accomplished.

Involve Your Children

As you start digging out of debt and making reasonable plans to get in control of your family finances, it is important to teach your children the value and benefit of financial planning. At a very young age, children can understand money. At ages three to five, you can teach your preschooler about receiving money and spending it wisely. Starting with a weekly allowance, the preschooler can begin to learn saving (in a piggy bank), tithing (10 percent of the allowance) to Sunday School, and making needed purchases.

At ages six to eight, you can give the child a slight increase in his allowance and start explaining money transactions, such as the amount of a restaurant tip, budgeting, and saving for that special purchase. A child at this age should have responsibilities in the home such as setting the table, making his or her bed, and feeding the family pet. While some parents feel that allowances should be given only if responsibilities are met, others feel the allowance is what the child is "allowed" to have. You have to decide what is best for your home.

At ages nine to eleven, you can increase the child's allowance and their home responsibilities in order to receive this. For example, you might require that your child keep his room clean, carry out the garbage daily, and walk the family pet. At this age, you can bring them into the family budget process to get their input when saving for that special vacation or summer camp. You might consider paying for certain chores that go beyond basic responsibilities, such as lawn mowing, weeding flower beds, washing windows, and babysitting.

Young teens, ages twelve to fourteen, can complement their allowance with outside jobs—babysitting, mowing lawns for neighbors, or even helping a neighbor with household chores. This early introduction into employment allows the young teen to feel important and gives him additional funds to save for large purchases.

Work Is Not a Bad Word for Teens

Many teenagers ages fifteen and up work part-time outside the home to earn money. Gloria, the parent of a sixteen-year-old, told of her daughter coming home one afternoon excited about a new part-time job. "After she explained the job description and agreed to our conditions, we gave her our approval," Gloria said. "We thought that the job would benefit Peggy in many ways, provided she maintained good grades, had no Sunday or night work, and did not work more than ten hours per week."

After six months on the job Gloria agreed that the job was a positive step for her daughter. "Peggy gets paid about fifty dollars per week. She sets aside five dollars to cover her tithe and savings, then gives us ten dollars toward her car insurance and gas. The rest she spends on clothing, CD's, and movies. Peggy now organizes her time better and is more disciplined with her homework."

While teenagers have great capacity for earning money at part-time jobs, they also know how to spend money with zeal. But parents can help! Here are a few rules you must know to help teens manage their extra income.

Making Money

Over six million teens in the United States work, with a median weekly earning of $83.37, according to recent figures from the Bureau of Labor Statistics.[1] Besides learning job skills, teens who work part-time jobs learn to be on time, get along with the public, and take orders from an adult who is not a parent.

Educators feel that the problem with a teen working part-time comes when the hours get excessive and he is no longer able to keep up in school. "It is important that parents monitor the teen who works outside the home so he can stay on task with schoolwork," a school principal said. "If the teen cannot handle both job and school assignments, the job should wait until summer months."

Budgeting Money

As you teach your teen how to handle money, help him set up a weekly and monthly budget. If your teen earns forty dollars a week doing odd jobs and babysitting, he should set aside half of this amount for a mandatory savings account with four dollars of this amount going toward his church tithe. This mandatory savings account can be designated toward a college fund, a big trip during summer months, or a used car. This will leave him twenty dollars per week to spend on clothes, movies, dates, or other teen necessities.

Sandy, the mother of two older teens, said, "Budgeting has worked great for my daughters as they look ahead at upcoming events and learn how to save extra money for that something special. If a school dance or community concert is coming up that month and the cost exceeds their weekly spending allowance, they know they have to save some each week to pay for this extra activity."

This budgeted savings helps teens learn how to prolong pleasure as they wait patiently for their reward—a good lesson in life.

Have your teen learn to budget by keeping track of where and how he spends his money for several weeks. A small notebook and calculator are essential as he keeps accurate records of his expenses. After a few weeks, your teen can look over his expenses and see where his money has gone. Is he spending too much on junk food? Video games? Movies?

Encourage your teen to take a piece of paper and write down two columns: the "Needs" and the "Wants." Needs might include savings for clothes, college, a car, or trip during the summer months. Wants might include an upcoming ski trip with his church youth group, a new sweater, or the latest CDs.

Once your teen has evaluated his spending and set goals for the upcoming months, he can adjust his budget accordingly— saving for "Needs" and deciding which "Wants" he must have (see sample Teen Budget). Setting spending priorities is an important lesson as your teen organizes what is important to him and puts money aside for this.

Spending Money

Should parents have a say in how a teen spends his money? Yes, we emphatically say.

Parents can:

➤ Plan a budget together—as a family.
➤ Talk with your teen about large purchases you make.
➤ Let him know the amount of money the family spends each week on food, necessities, and bills.
➤ Cut coupons together as a family for weekly meals.

You do not need to reveal every detail of your income or debts, but as your teen sees you staying on a family budget, he can gain skills in budgeting his personal income.

Parents must also discourage impulse spending with teens. Encourage your teen to review his goals and budget before he goes to the mall with friends. Knowing ahead of time how much "mad money" he has to spend will help keep your teen responsible.

Money Does Matter to Teens

Teen savings accounts are available at most banks around the nation. Joint accounts with the parent usually have no bank fees and can accumulate interest. You can even open a savings account with a joint signature so the teen has access to the money only with your consent.

Money does matter to teens today. Especially in tough economic times when families are tightening their belts, teens must be taught financial responsibility. Just like in every other facet of living, parents can teach teens how to be responsible caretakers of their income, encourage tithing and saving, and lead the way at home with careful spending.

Sample Teen Budget

NEEDS	WANTS
Church tithe	Cokes after school
College fund	New CD
Insurance for car	Movie on Friday night
Math computer program	Video game

Weekly income: $40.00   Weekly expenses: $40.00

Church tithe: 4.00

Savings: 16.00

Spending: 20.00

Calculating Your Net Worth

As you get on the road to taking control of your finances, you need to determine your net worth. Net worth is your assets (what you own) less your liabilities (what you owe). Net worth is a way to determine your financial health and should be recomputed on a regular basis—at least annually—to measure progress in achieving financial security. Net worth shows your ability to withstand any setback with your income, cover unexpected expenses, college expenses, retirement, and more. Your net worth should grow faster than inflation and be able to meet whatever goals you set up. You can compare your net worth with the table below to see how you compare with the median net worth by age and income.

Net Worth by Age and Income

Annual Household Income

AGE	$20,400–30,799	$30,800–46,599	$46,600–up
16-34	6,440	15,420	37,817
35-44	20,008	39,983	88,293
45-54	38,295	65,794	130,867
55-64	84,267	96,066	198,987
65-up	141,811	201,562	343,015

SOURCE:
U.S. Census Bureau. Does not include insurance, pensions, or personal assets.

3-Year Net Worth Worksheet

Net worth worksheet for: _____

Date: _____

ASSETS (What you own)	Current	Year 2	Year 3
1. Total Bank funds: (checking, M.M.,C.D.'s)	_____	_____	_____
2. Investments (Stocks, Mutual funds etc.)	_____	_____	_____
3. Other Investments (Real Estate, Coins)			

	Current	Year 2	Year 3
4. Net value of business	_____	_____	_____
5. Insurance cash value	_____	_____	_____
6. Automobiles (market value)	_____	_____	_____
7. Retirement Plan (I.R.A.,401K, etc.)	_____	_____	_____
8. Residence (market value)	_____	_____	_____
9. Other assets (notes owed you, etc.)	_____	_____	_____
10. TOTAL ASSETS	_____	_____	_____

LIABILITIES
(What you owe)

	Current	Year 2	Year 3
11. Mortgage(s) (balance owed)	_____	_____	_____
12. Auto loans	_____	_____	_____
13. Other loans	_____	_____	_____
14. Monthly bills (credit cards, etc.)	_____	_____	_____
15. Other debts	_____	_____	_____
16. TOTAL LIABILITIES	(_____)	(_____)	(_____)
NET WORTH (assets minus liabilities)	_____	_____	_____

How Do Your Expenses Compare?

The Bureau of Labor Statistics has established typical ranges for each expense category (see the chart on the page following). Use these percentages as a guide to establish your budget. For example, in housing some families spend as little as 20 percent of their yearly income, with others spending up to 31 percent.

Knowing these typical ranges gives you a broad range to adjust your own expenses. For example, maybe you could reduce debt by 5 percent and move this 5 percent to the savings. Or as a challenge, you might try to reduce all expenses by a total of 10 percent, move this to savings, and watch it compound for years. When this happens, your financial security will take off.

Category	Percentage of Take Home Pay
Housing	20 to 31
Food (at home and out)	14 to 30
Debt repayment (incl. car loans)	10 to 20
Transportation	6 to 20
Clothing	3 to 10
Savings	5 to 9
Health and Medical	2 to 8
Insurance	4 to 9
Utilities	4 to 7
Tithe and donations	3 to 11

Develop Budget Goals

When you fill out the quarterly budget worksheet on the next page, you will get a good idea of where your money is going. The following steps will assist you in gathering the information and listing it on the worksheets given. Use a monthly average of the past three months on these variable expenses. For annual expenses paid less frequently, total these for the year, then divide by twelve for the monthly average. When you compute the ongoing monthly actual, list the monthly amount. This budget can be your plan for a successful future as you work on the income and expenses, then revise the totals until you gain control of your finances.

Three Month Work Sheet

Quarterly Budget Worksheet for _____

Date_____

Category	Goal	Month 1	Month 2	Month 3
INCOME				
Wages & Salary	_____	_____	_____	_____
Investment	_____	_____	_____	_____
Interest	_____	_____	_____	_____
Other	_____	_____	_____	_____
Total Income	_____	_____	_____	_____
EXPENSE				
Allowances	_____	_____	_____	_____
Automobile				
payments	_____	_____	_____	_____
gasoline	_____	_____	_____	_____
maintenance	_____	_____	_____	_____
donations	_____	_____	_____	_____
(tithe, other)				
Child-care	_____	_____	_____	_____
Clothing	_____	_____	_____	_____
Education	_____	_____	_____	_____
(tuition,books, etc.)				
Food				
dining out	_____	_____	_____	_____
groceries	_____	_____	_____	_____
Furnishings	_____	_____	_____	_____
Gifts	_____	_____	_____	_____
Healthcare				
dental	_____	_____	_____	_____
medical	_____	_____	_____	_____
Housing				
mortgage	_____	_____	_____	_____
maintenance	_____	_____	_____	_____
rent	_____	_____	_____	_____

	Goal	Month 1	Month 2	Month 3
Insurance				
automobile	_____	_____	_____	_____
health	_____	_____	_____	_____
homeowner's	_____	_____	_____	_____
renter's	_____	_____	_____	_____
life	_____	_____	_____	_____
Interest expense				
mortgage intr.	_____	_____	_____	_____
other	_____	_____	_____	_____
Job expenses	_____	_____	_____	_____
Leisure/recr.	_____	_____	_____	_____
Miscellaneous	_____	_____	_____	_____
Personal care	_____	_____	_____	_____
Savings/invest.	_____	_____	_____	_____
Total Expense	_____	_____	_____	_____

Income

To begin tallying your net worth, start by breaking down your current income (net after income and Social Security tax deductions) from payroll stubs, including overtime, commissions, and known bonuses. List this monthly average in the space provided. Break down other income into monthly averages and list accordingly. Now total the income column and list this total. Continue to follow these instructions as you total your net worth.

Expenses

➤ Allowances: Show monthly amount for expense.
➤ Automobile: List actual note payment(s).
  List average of past three months gasoline and maintenance expenses.
➤ Charitable: List the monthly tithe on first line; all others on second.
➤ Childcare: List monthly average.
➤ Clothing: List monthly average.

➤ Education: Compute annual tuition. Divide this by twelve, plus the average for books and supplies, etc.

➤ Food: Use three months average.

➤ Furnishings: Use average of past twelve months.

➤ Gifts: Use average past twelve months.

➤ Healthcare: Average past three months for health/dental (non-insurance premium costs).

➤ Housing: List payment of principal for mortgage; average for maintenance; actual for rent.

➤ Insurance: Use one-twelfth of annual for auto, homeowners, renters, and life; monthly actual for health/dental.

➤ Interest: Mortgage/auto use actual. Recognize that this will change monthly.

➤ Other: Charge card/bank fees, etc.

➤ Job Expenses: Uniforms, dues; all job-related expenses.

➤ Leisure/recreation: Use past year expenses in order to include vacation; divide by twelve.

➤ Miscellaneous: Use actual monthly average for all other amounts not listed elsewhere.

➤ Personal Care: Use past three months average.

➤ Savings/Investments: Use past twelve months average.

After you run a total of each expense column, add up these expenses. The grand total of expenses should equal your total income.

Capitalize on the Housing Recovery, Smartly!

Owning a home is still part of the American dream, although with inflation very low and the effects of corporate cutbacks on real estate values, increases have flattened out in most areas of the country.

For the long term, you might consider home ownership as one of your goals as you gain control of your family income. You can still realize tax deductions on the interest and real estate taxes. From the lessons of the early nineties, you need to reevaluate your housing needs, fitting it into your long-term family goals.

After you determine your actual net worth and list your current monthly spending on the budget worksheet, study your results and compare with the median net worth for your peer group. Do you have adequate assets to cover a change in your income? It is recommended that you have an amount that would equal six months income for emergencies. Can you continue your lifestyle should your spouse be laid off? What would happen when you have children, and you cut back to one income? Will this cause upheaval in your plans?

Review differences in the amount of house payment and interest paid for different mortgage amounts. For example, if you settle on the $100,000 mortgage at 7 percent over thirty years instead of a budget-straining $150,000 mortgage, your payment would be $332.65 per month less than the $150,000 mortgage, or a savings of $3991.80 per year. If you then saved this amount, rounded to $4000 per year with compounding interest at 10 percent for thirty years, your nest egg would grow to a whopping $657,976.

Taking control of your family income takes sound planning, and setting reasonable goals and priorities. Realistic housing may help in your overall family planning.

As the following tables show, you can realize a significant savings by paying off your mortgage in a fifteen-year period of time. However, we suggest that you obtain a thirty-year mortgage. A thirty-year mortgage will have a slightly lower monthly payment for a safety net for future family emergencies, such as one spouse losing his job or not having this income available. As you do this, amortize the mortgage over a fifteen-year period of time as long as the family cash flow is available. If an emergency strikes, then you can fall back to the lower payment.

Another tip on your family's housing needs is that in some circumstances, buying your home may not be the best alternative. A prime example would be families in government service or construction workers who move to various job sites; renting may be the better alternative. A house is a nonliquid asset, and it may be hard to dispose of quickly. If you are transferred or your job ends suddenly, you may end up selling the home at a loss. Therefore, it would be wiser to rent on a temporary basis and then look to establish a homestead in the place or area where you want to retire.

The following charts will assist in helping determine the amount of interest payable on various mortgages and the effect of compounding interest on your savings.

Comparison of Interest Paid

at 15 Years vs. 30 Years at 7 Percent

Principal	Term	Payment	Total Payback	Total Interest
50,000	15	449.41	80,893.80	30,893.80
50,000	30	332.65	119,754.00	69,754.00
100,000	15	898.83	161,789.40	61,789.40
100,000	30	665.30	239,508.00	139,508.00
150,000	15	1348.24	242,683.20	92,683.20
150,000	30	997.95	359,262.00	209,262.00

Retirement Planning for the Young Family

If you read or listen to any financial advisor, somewhere in their presentation or book they will address the secret of wealth building called *compounding*. We all are familiar with savings accounts that draw a certain rate of interest, and the bank has interest that is compounded daily, quarterly, etc. The advantage of a retirement account is that not only does it compound, but it also is tax-deferred when placed in a qualified retirement plan, IRA, or 401-K plan.

Granted, at some point in the future, you will have to pay personal income tax on these monies. But, as history has shown, you are taking monies now, putting them aside before tax dollars; therefore the interest or the growth (the appreciation if you have mutual funds or stocks) that results from a retirement account is not only on your money, but on some of the money that should have gone to Uncle Sam in the way of income taxes. At the end of your retirement, of course, you are going to have to pay the taxes, but you have had, in effect, a tax free loan from Uncle Sam for twenty, thirty or forty years—during your active work career.

This discipline of contributing the maximum amount of monies that you can to your profit-sharing plan is necessary for financial control. (If it has contributory features, your 401-K plan is matched by your employer. So if you do not contribute, you are virtually giving money away or back to your employer.) Of most importance is that people tend to live on or spend what they have in their take-home pay. If the monies are taken out in advance, you will never miss them and your lifestyle, and spending habits will adjust.

The advantage of starting off immediately in your work career of funding an IRA—or if you are self-employed a simplified employee pension (SEP) plan— is that when the time comes to purchase your house, pending legislation may allow the early withdrawal without penalty to purchase your house. Second, by having a liquid IRA or 401-K plan, you are building an emergency reserve. If you should become unemployed, ill, or have family emergencies, the habit that you start now in your early career will carry on through your life.

The table on the next page shows how an IRA can compound. Before long, you will have the security of knowing that besides social security, you will have additional monies in your retirement account. Paying the church tithe first (10 percent of your income), then paying yourself second (savings, IRA, SEP, 401-K plan or other) will mean the difference between a secure family life and one that is insecure.

The earlier you begin funding your savings plan, the harder compounding works for you. If you start at age twenty-five and fund your wealth builder at 8 percent interest for ten years and stop— but leave the fund compounding at 8 percent interest until age sixty-five—you would have amassed $291,547! On the other hand, if you wait to start at age 35 and fund for the next thirty years $2000 per year at 8 percent interest you would only amass only $226,566, some $65,000 less than funding for twenty years more. This shows the importance of starting as early as possible and letting compounding work for you.

SAVINGS WITH BEFORE-TAX DOLLARS
(CURRENT TAX BRACKETS: 15%, 28%, 31%, 36%, 39.6%)

There is a difference in the yield of a savings account made up of before-tax dollars as opposed to after tax dollars. Consider:

Before-tax Dollars:
At age thirty, if you start saving $2,000 before-tax dollars per year at 10 percent interest and save for thirty years, you would have $328,988. If you saved $4,000 for the same thirty years at 10 percent, you would have $657,976.

After-tax Dollars:

Amount	Tax Bracket	Tax	Net Saving	Amount in 30 Years
$2000	15%	$300	$1700	$279,640
$2000	28%	$560	$1440	$236,871
$2000	31%	$620	$1380	$227,002
$2000	36%	$720	$1280	$210,552
$2000	39.6%	$792	$1208	$198,709
$4000	39.6%	$1584	$2416	$397,417

Save Money and Pay Yourself

The median American household allocates each dollar of their net worth as follows:

Housing, other real estate . . . . $.54

Savings 14

Stocks, mutual funds. .07

Business 07

Saving bonds, other investments. 065

Cars trucks 06

Retirement accounts 05

Checking. 005

(Source: U.S. Census Bureau)

Some very wealthy people have discovered early the importance of compounding interest. Other people play the game. When you make any purchase on an installment plan or credit card, such as appliances, gifts, clothes, automobiles, and even a home, these purchases are not completely paid for. The merchants have discovered that financing your purchase at interest up to 18 percent or more offers more profit than they make off the sale of the item.

Everywhere we turn the advertising is directed at making us want the product and showing how easy and painless the payments are. For example, if you have a $2,000 balance on your credit card at 18 percent interest, requiring a minimum payment of 2.5 percent of the balance, you would pay $50 per month. If you decide to pay this off at the minimum amount over five years and not add to the account, you would pay $50.79 each month. At the end of one year, you would have paid in $609.47, total with interest eating up $338.35. The balance owed would only be reduced to $1728.87. At the end of five years you would have paid $3,047.40 to pay off the $2,000.00 balance; of this $1,047.40 would be in interest.

You can see why the finance company so generously permits you to pay the minimum amount. Can you imagine owing $4,000, $8,000, or more on total credit cards each month? One family told of owing more than $15,000 on eight major credit cards. If they paid off their cards over five years at 18 percent interest, they would pay $380.90 per month, for a total of $22,854.00. The interest alone amounted to $7,854.00.

If you are a hostage to the easy credit of the plastic card, you are not alone. But you need to understand the debts you have incurred. Credit card interest is not tax deductible; therefore, when you pay this interest, you are paying with after-tax dollars. In the 28 percent tax bracket, it takes $1.39 in wages or other income to pay each $1.00 of credit card or other purchases.

For the family that has already fallen into the credit card trap, consider plastic surgery. This means that you take out the scissors and cut up all of your credit cards except for one—one universal card such as MasterCard or Visa. This one card then should be stored in the very back of your wallet and never used. Commit to start paying cash for every item. The reason that you will need one card is for emergency needs, such as if you are traveling away from home and are unable to cash a personal check or need to go into a walk-in clinic or have emergency car repairs. But again, once you have performed plastic surgery, use the card "only in an emergency."

Are You Gaining Control?

The National Center for Financial Education says the key to saving is controlling spending. The center's profile of a good spender is someone who: [2]

➤ Keeps a small amount of cash from each paycheck.
➤ Deposits money each payday into a checking and savings account.
➤ Sets aside money for fixed expenses such as mortgages and 10 percent for savings after getting a paycheck.
➤ Sticks to a written spending plan.
➤ Plans all grocery shopping with a list and rarely goes to the grocery store more than once a week.
➤ Uses grocery coupons.
➤ Comparison shops.
➤ Carries no credit card balances.
➤ Has no outstanding loans except a mortgage.
➤ Comparison-shops auto insurance once a year.
➤ Dines out only once a week.
➤ Has received statements estimating Social Security and pension benefits.
➤ Can account for all cash spent at the end of each day.
➤ Belongs to a credit union.
➤ Automatically invests a set amount of money each month.
➤ Saves paycheck stubs.
➤ Gives regularly to the needy.

Millions of Americans have vowed to gain control over their income, but getting into this habit does not happen overnight. As you set your family budget, remember to:

➤ Set realistic goals.
➤ Communicate openly with all family members.
➤ Ask for God's help to resist the buying temptations.
➤ Pray daily for the wisdom to turn your family's finances around.

As you gain control of your family's income, establish a deeper relationship with God, for He has the power to change your priorities. But you still must take action such as cutting up credit cards and limiting purchases to only those items budgeted that you can pay cash for. Look at the following steps that will help you gain control:

➤ Go back over the past year and list your spending. You will see that many purchases were spur-of-the-moment, impulsive decisions. Eliminate unnecessary spending and work out a goal for each budget item.

➤ Make a shopping list, and ask, "Do I really need this?" Stick to your list.

➤ Clip coupons, but do not purchase just because you have the coupon. Do you really need it? Compare it with store brands.

➤ Shop wholesale clubs for larger quantities and save up to 30 to 40 percent.

➤ Buy clothes at season's end and on sale when possible.

➤ Shop discount department stores, factory outlets, and always compare quality and price. You will find the more an item is advertised, the more it costs.

➤ Shop garage sales, when possible, in the higher income neighborhoods. Many times you will find high quality children's clothes at one-tenth of the new cost.

➤ Shop thrift shops. You can find clothing, appliances, and furniture that may be in excellent condition for low cost.

➤ Custom-make your children's clothes. Take a sewing course and find out how easy it is.

➤ Contact your utility company for an energy audit. Many companies will do this at no charge or at least no more than a few dollars. Some will even offer a rebate for you to upgrade to a more efficient heating and cooling system. Insulate your hot water heater and check into the possibility of a timer to heat water only when you need it. Become aware of the energy efficiency of all appliances. Tremendous savings, up to 40 to 50 percent can be found over old heating and cooling systems and appliances. Install low-flow shower heads and aerators.

➤ Look at your automobiles. The family that buys top-of-the-line cars every three years is making a costly mistake in keeping up with the Joneses. Sam Walton, one of the richest men in our country, was famous for sporting around town in his used pickup truck. Tremendous savings may be possible in reviewing transportation needs. Review *Consumer Reports* for the best value in making this large purchase; in fact, you should check this source before all major purchases.

You might decide to have only one family car, with others depending on city transportation. Or you might purchase a low mileage car. A new car drops in value up to 30 percent when it is driven off the dealer's lot. Today most dealers have program cars, from rental programs with low mileage at up to 35 percent, and discounts off current models with several years factory warranty left. Compare with a new car, and negotiate the price and interest rate, if financed. After several years, the older car can become the second car. Consider driving it for as long as it provides sound transportation.

➤ Take advantage of the many opportunities your church offers for fellowship. Covered dish meals, youth fellowships, church camp, retreats, Sunday School parties, singles fellowships and more are free and will help you grow in your Christian commitment. We compared summer camps and found our denomination's youth camp was one-fourth the cost of a private camp— in the same area in North Carolina with the same activities but with a spiritual emphasis.

➤ Consider vacations at church recreation facilities. Most denominations have different campgrounds and retreat centers available for members.

➤ Review insurance coverage with your agent and consider increasing your deductibles on auto, homeowners, or renters up to $500 or more.

➤ If you are working part-time with children in day-care, consider a co-op with other parents who also work part-time. Schedule your work to make the co-op work and save the day-care cost.

➤ Become computer literate as there are many inexpensive software programs to assist in personal financial planning and budgeting.

➤ Explore the availability of purchasing food co-ops through your church or neighborhood groups.

➤ Make meals from scratch; reduce prepared dishes; minimize restaurant meals and call-in pizzas.

➤ When these changes are not enough, consider lifestyle changes. Move to a smaller house or plan for additional education to qualify for a more lucrative position.

➤ Subscribe to a magazine that offers tips on money management. *Consumer Reports* and *Money* magazine are worth considering. Some excellent resources for financial management include: Larry Burkett's *Answers to Your Family's Financial Questions*; Jane Bryant Quinn's *Making the Most of Your Money*; and Joe Dominguez and Vicki Robin's *Your Money or Your Life*.

Living on One Income

Living on the income from one spouse is an achievable goal if the entire family makes the commitment to that goal. We all know or have heard of large families where only one parent works. The secret to success of living on one income is working together. Peer pressure often determines the family lifestyle and what expenditures the family makes. Living on one income means adhering to a strict budget.

The first step is the listing of your income and expenses and tracking these expenses on a monthly basis. The next step involves setting goals and looking at the items that can be reduced. Commitment to these goals by all family members is essential. The family should first budget the basic housing, food, and clothing needs. Take advantage of any programs that are offered by your church or local agencies. A meeting with a home economist can provide you with useful ways of meeting your family's basic needs within the community which you live, or they can point you to other social agencies that provide free resources to you. You should be aware that you are the one who is responsible, and once you make an effort to commit and work hard toward these goals, you can achieve living on one income.

Next, evaluate your educational needs and technical skills. Both you or your spouse may have to pay to obtain some additional education or technical training so that you can boost your income. Education is a continuing process, and in today's market and the world economy, we can never stop learning.

According to the Department of Labor, most people will have four to five different jobs within their lifetime. This is not the same position that our parents or grandparents were in, where they could count on remaining at one job for twenty years and retiring with a good pension. You are responsible for maintaining your educational skills, and these educational skills will help you to achieve your goal of living on one family income.

The young family just starting out should seriously consider family planning and how soon they will have children. The three major expenditures in any family's life are their home, car, and children. If you can defer having children for a period of time and build a basic foundation in your family model such as your housing needs, it will be much easier to have one spouse remain at home during the important first five years of your child's development.

The spouse that remains at home still can supplement the family income if, through their educational training, he or she has developed good skills. Secretarial work, bookkeeping, or even freelance writing can be done in the home if the person understands basic word processing programs. Other kinds of home-based businesses that might supplement the family income include telemarketing, baby-sitting, filing services, caring for the elderly, tutoring, offering piano or writing lessons, and more. Many employers are taking advantage of a home-based work environment, as the person is able to efficiently work using a personal computer, modem, and fax machine.

A word of caution: You can create your own business at home yourself, so avoid those advertisements telling you to "buy" a home-based business. For a very minimal investment, your local public library contains books that will guide you on this plan. The personal financial planning section and business opportunity section of your bookstore can also show you books on how to begin. By doing the research and taking inventory of your skills and knowledge, a spouse staying at home can supplement the family's income.

Living on one income can be done. If you feel this would benefit your family, check your budget and set some short- and long-term goals so it can be a reality in the not-too-distant future.

Investment Planning

Investment planning for the family starts once the basic needs for the family have been met and the family has started putting funds away for retirement. A wealth of information is available in helping you meet your investment goals.

One should become familiar with the investment triangle. The broad base or strong foundation of the triangle is your home. Your retirement is the next section of the triangle. Then the family should consider stock and bonds. The question of how you get into stocks and bonds can be answered in a whole book or hundreds of books. The family that is new to the investing posture should do research and get involved with mutual funds, which is based on the philosophy of not putting all your eggs in one basket and allowing professional money managers and advisors to lead you through this learning experience.

When you read any literature or surveys on building wealth or when the wealthiest people in the nation are interviewed, there are two areas where they expect primarily to build or create additional wealth: in real estate and in the stock market.

The stock market is a two-edged sword. When a wealthy individual speaks of the stock market, he might also be talking about the stock options that are associated directly with the business that he owns or has created in letting these stocks go public. This avenue is not available to the average family and is a high-risk venture far beyond the scope of this book. We are talking about building a basic philosophy or foundation.

If you look at the traditional returns, a good home—or as you are able, trading up to a nicer home and keeping the additional home as rental property—can provide cash flow that can service your investments. You can also take a certain amount of your savings and put it into mutual funds, but you must always consider the risk that is associated with it. Once stockbrokers and insurance agents are aware that you are investing, your name inevitably gets on mailing lists, and you get calls from people who are willing to sell you almost anything.

One of the strong sales techniques is the tax-sheltering effect that any investment might have. In our past experience with many individuals, the person that invests only to save income taxes or lets the tax dog wag the investment usually comes out as the loser. These products are only made to market, not to grow and offer an economic return.

For the person who is first getting involved with extra disposable funds, the safest item is the stock market through mutual funds. Traditionally, the market since the early 1900s has returned between 10 and 11 percent on the investment. If you steadily put monies aside and diversify them into various types of funds, as we spoke of earlier, a 10 percent return compounded over a thirty-year period can lead to significant financial security. It is making that first step of freeing up funds to invest, not save, that is intimidating.

A distinction must be made here. As you gain control of your income, save first to meet emergency needs and second for that six-month financial reserve that a family should have. Investing should be your next means of savings, as you pick items that will grow and add to your financial security and wealth over a long period of time.

Sick, Dead, or Old

One of these, and usually all three, will happen to everyone in their lifetime. Each of these occurrences has an economic impact on someone, whether it be one person or the family. Therefore, it is the responsibility of the head of the family to insure the coverage of each eventuality.

Obviously, there is a cost involved. Each family has to determine the amount needed and affordability of each. That does not suggest postponement of taking care of all or some of the problem.

Let's look at each of the three problems.

Sickness. No one, young or old is immune from disease of the body. The cost of health care has been skyrocketing over the years. Right now there are a few ways to insure our health cost. This can be done through individual health insurance, which is sometimes very expensive and hard to get all members to qualify. To keep the cost down you have to have high deductibles.

Groups, small or large, have the best and usually the most inexpensive cost of coverage. Usually the small groups are classified under ten lives. Most companies now pool all groups under twenty-five lives. Large groups are quoted each year on their own merit.

The types of plans are the following:

➤ PPO (Preferred Provider Organization): That means you will go to physicians and hospitals that are contracted with the insurance company. They will pay the largest percentage to the PPO. If you go outside the plan to another hospital or physician, your percentage of coverage is usually 20 percent less.

➤ HMO (Health Maintenance Organization):This plan's coverage is only for those hospitals and physicians contracted with the HMO companies. Outside coverage is only for emergencies. This really limits where you go and who you see.

➤ Regular comprehensive plans are generally standard group plans but have less percentage of coverage than the other two plans. However, you can go to any physician or hospital. Many companies will provide PPO and comprehensive plans within the same group.

Another help for the sick person is disability income, better known as income replacement. This will protect a portion of one's income in case of total or partial disability. This usually has waiting periods of 30 to 180 days before the income begins. The longer you are not working and producing income the greater the length of the waiting period. The benefit period usually runs from one year to age sixty-five.

Long Term Care has entered the market, mainly for the elderly. This provides coverage for nursing care and home care. Most people wait until they are near retirement before taking on the extra cost. However, the older you are, the more expensive it gets. People should consider it at a lower age to control cost; coverage is offered for groups and individuals.

Death. This is not a question of "if" but "when" death will occur. Knowing this, the family should make plans to ensure the one or ones that contribute to the economic needs of the family. Life insurance is for the living not the dead. A person should want the family to live in their own world, not to have to change their place, friends, or standard of living. Families do not mind the cost of covering home and auto, probably because in most instances it is required; this will still be required when the head of the household dies. Life insurance premiums per thousand are the only products on the market today where the cost has gone down instead of up as people live healthier and longer.

The type of plan depends on many things such as need, ability to pay, and type of plan. There are different types of plans depending on your needs. A term plan can give a lot of coverage with a small premium outlay; however, it gets expensive as you get into later years. Most plans end by age seventy.

You can convert to more permanent coverage such as whole life, universal life, or adjustable life. These permanent plans give you coverage with a part of the premium going into a cash value or cash reserve. The cash build-up can be looked on as a form of forced savings and can also be used as part of your cash reserves. In later years, it can be helpful for college funding, to pay off loans, or for retirement income. This method can save plus insure one's life.

Aged. Assume one has been fortunate enough to reach retirement age. That means in most instances the working income has stopped, but the need to provide the necessities of life goes on. Social Security was set in motion in 1937 to take care of that problem; and now it plays only a small part. A person needs to supplement Social Security in order to live the life as it was before retirement.

In order to do that, you need for retirement an income that will provide at least 60 to 80 percent of what was produced before retirement. This is with the Social Security income as part of the percentage. How does one get it? Most get income from pension or profit-sharing plans where they were employed, normally providing 60 percent. If you need more, you can enroll in other plans the company provides, such as 401-K, Deferred Compensation, Tax-deferred Plans, savings plans, or your own permanent life insurance and personal investing.

People are creatures of habit, and good habits will determine your success. Start by investing on a regular basis so that you and your family can enjoy a secure life later.

The Will Is for Everyone

When you become an adult and start building your own estate—and even more so when you have a spouse and/or children— you need a will. Still, up to 60 percent of all adults do not have a will. This can be one of the most important decisions an adult can make. Without a will the court will decide how to divide your estate, and it will take a very long time to do so at tremendous cost.

A simple will should cost between $100 and $300 and should be drawn up by an attorney. A properly drawn will is important to carry out your instructions upon your death. Other estate planning tools such as joint ownership and living trusts could increase the cost somewhat, but the results are still cost effective. Review your will periodically as your estate changes or when you move to another state.

It Is Up to You!

Getting control of your family income is important to reclaiming your family. As you understand where your money is coming from and where it has been going, you can make some intentional changes and begin to allocate your resources more responsibly. You will be able to achieve some lifelong goals and dreams for your family as you gain control of finances.

Family Time

1. At a family meeting talk with your children about the responsibilities of money. Have them make a list with two columns on a sheet of paper. On one side, ask them to list all of the "needs" they spend money on, including savings account, church tithe, clothes, school supplies, and gas or car insurance (if teen driver). On the other side ask them to list all of the "wants" they spend money on such as coloring books or cassette tapes, bubble gum and colas, movies and video games, etc. Talk with your children about the difference between "needs" and "wants." Tell them how God will take care of all our "needs," but this is different than our "wants." Help them to establish a priority system with their weekly allowance so their "needs" will be taken care of, and encourage them to postpone instant gratification by saving for their "wants."

2. Using the checklist on page 211, talk with your family about ways to cut back on spending. Choose one night each week where children cut out coupons from current magazines or newspapers, and use these while shopping for groceries. Talk with your children about the importance of recycling clothes and other items instead of always wanting something "new."

Look through a current magazine and discuss the advertisements for products such as makeup, clothing, CD and book clubs, etc. Show your children how advertisers try to manipulate consumers, and encourage them to be selective shoppers.

Notes

1. "Teens and Money," *Ladies Home Journal* (September1991), 138.

2. "Good Spenders," *Florida Times-Union* (February 13, 1994), G-1.

Chapter 7

Take Control
of the Media

Growing up begins earlier than ever before in our nation. Think about when you were a child. What occupied your time at ages three, eight, and eleven?

Thirty years ago, a three-year-old would spend the day pulling her red wagon filled with blocks; today she wears "pretend" makeup while playing with a shapely fashion doll and miniature sports car. An eight-year-old used to play kickball with a neighborhood gang; now he spends afternoons locked in his room, absorbed in his video games. And a thirteen-year-old who used to innocently enter the teen years now speaks with pseudomaturity about such topics as homosexuality, AIDS and sexually transmitted diseases—with information he learned not from his parents but from MTV. Has the media robbed our children of their childhood?

Thirty years ago, parents took pride in protecting children from growing up too fast, holding them back from conversations and suggestions that were too "adult." We remember our parents having stern rules about which movies we could see with friends and even walking out of movies if they were too suggestive. Three decades ago, parents decided what they would tell their children about life's lessons and when they would do this. But sadly enough, many parents today are allowing total strangers—celebrated actors on television and movies, revered rock singers, popular sports heros, and more—to tell their children what is most important in life. To be perfectly honest, the messages our children are being given by the media are usually not what we want them to hear.

Who Will Teach Our Children?

When our oldest son was in fourth grade, he was very impressed by the popular karate videos, and, in fact, took karate lessons for a while so he could be like a "ninja." All of this seemed quite innocent to us until Rob began to try his new maneuvers on his sisters—in an aggressive manner that certainly was not civilized. While he knew that the karate "chops" the actors did in the movies were fake, he did not know where to draw the line in the reality of home life. Needless to say, after a quick karate chop into his younger sister's arm, we dropped the lessons and the movies for awhile until he gained the maturity needed to use these skills in a responsible manner.

Because Rob is now a solid young adult, we can tell his story and use these illustrations to show the impact the media has upon our children. After watching a rerun of "Saturday Night Fever" with John Travolta, eleven-year-old Rob decided to become a break dancer. You can imagine our shock when we returned home from a dinner engagement, and our trusted baby-sitter (Rob) had thickly coated the kitchen floor with cooking oil so that he and his sisters could "spin" like in the movie.

We could provide you with entire book of personal accounts on how impressionable children and teens are, but the point is clear: Parents have a vital responsibility in this age of mass communication to evaluate every form of media that touches the lives of their children. As you reclaim the family, you can teach children to make objective decisions with the media, including television shows, movies, videos, and music. Using some practical screening methods with your family, you can ensure that the messages your children are receiving are consistent with the family's morals, values, and beliefs. While many claim that we are becoming a fragmented MTV-rock video generation, there is great hope for those families who start to take control.

Controlling the Television

When our neighbor came by and commented that her family had "cut the plug" on their television set, we honestly thought she had lost her mind. "TV has taken control of our lives," she explained. "So rather than watch our kids sit and stare at the set for hours each day this summer, we have simply made it unavailable. Now no one can turn it on."

In our family we have considered "pulling the plug" on this so-called electronic baby-sitter. But when we really think about the advantages verses the perils, this marvelous multi-channel communicator prevails every time.

Now television does have many drawbacks, especially considering its violence and graphic depiction of sex, but don't forget the excellent programming and news reporting it offers. In fact, in our home we enjoy spending some of our leisure time in front of the set. With a switch of the button we can travel to faraway countries, visit Nashville's Grand Ole Opry, or sit in the catcher's position for our favorite team. When we choose to turn on our set, we discover the latest in medical techniques, keep abreast of the political development abroad, or listen to a symphony on the public television network. And all these experiences can be ours without spending money.

The Key Word Is "Choice"

In a nation with more than 160 million TV sets flickering in living rooms seven hours a day, the key word for everyone as they watch TV is choice.[1] Just as we carefully choose what we read or eat or whom we imitate, we guide our three children in carefully selecting programs on the television. And these programs have generated positive ideas about the world around us that we could have never given to them.

Problems arise in homes where choice and discretion are not used regarding television. Take thirteen-year-old Kerrie, for example. Kerrie lets herself into her home after school and props in front of the television until 6:30 when her mother comes home. That is three hours of television. She then helps her mother clean up the kitchen after dinner and proceeds to do her homework—in front of the television—from 7:30 until 9:30. Every day this healthy teenager watches five hours of television—over one-sixth of her day is spent sitting in front of a TV—receiving no interaction with friends, no exercise, and no intimate talks with Mom to build their relationship.

The sad fact is that Kerrie is not a lone statistic; she represents millions of children across the nation who have no limits on television, with some modest reports telling of children viewing an average of three to five hours of television daily. Some studies even say that by high school graduation, the average teen will have spent more time watching television than in the classroom. Other studies reveal that teachers believe at least 25 percent of their students are not getting enough sleep because of late-evening TV.

While watching TV is entertaining and relaxing for some, having a steady diet of television shuts down a child's creative prowess and motivation for learning.

Does the Television Run Your Life?

How can I get people to like me?
What if my friends think this haircut is stupid?
Why don't my parents understand me?

Families, churches, schools, and neighborhoods used to provide the resources to help young people discover the answers to their questions; but today, movies, television, and music provide the information and the role models.

"We are a nation of people sitting around in the evening watching television," says Quentin J. Schultze, professor of communication arts and sciences at Calvin College in Grand Rapids, Michigan.

Schultze tells parents that the "only way to cope is to develop interpersonal relationships that are so healthy and so authentic that your child's need to reach out to the media and even, to some extent, to peers is not so strong."[2]

Are the Values on TV Your Values?

The effect of a steady diet of television on our children may not surface for many years, but do your children receive their values from the television shows they watch each day?

Let's reflect again to childhood days. Most children three decades ago spent their evenings reading books and maybe watching one well-chosen television show with their family. Of course, not many television programs were "off limits" then as most were produced for a "general audience." In other words, they had decency.

Remember the "Mary Tyler Moore Show"? She and her TV husband, Dick Van Dyke, slept in separate beds to keep their ratings high. During this period, if a married couple slept in the same bed, they had to show their feet out of the covers to get approved for television! Compare this with today—at any given moment on national cable television, your child can flip the channels to watch seductive sexual scenes—without your permission.

Watch Your Daytime Programming

The soap operas are an excellent example of this degeneration. Each day on national daytime networks, soap operas are available for the viewer with all the themes of the nineties—incest, adultery, children out of wedlock, drug and alcohol problems. The sad truth is that the ratings for soap operas are at an all-time high— people spend their afternoons glued to the set, absorbing the story and viewing the seduction. How many people begin to act out in real life the daytime dramas they have seen? Perhaps television is where some adults get their values today.

Television Can Be a Stumbling Block

The problem with our infatuation with television is that our Christian values are not reinforced by the media in our culture, making it impossible at times to reclaim the family. When children spend more time listening to the television than to their parents or teachers, regaining control of the family is difficult. While it may seem easy to allow children to keep company with the TV, this convenience often becomes another stumbling block in the child's maturation and personal development. And the messages children receive from some programs are not consistent with the message of the Christian family.

In a May 1993 survey 1,015 adults, ages eighteen and older, were polled on their television viewing habits. Here are their responses:

Quality of programming has decreased 57%

Don't like the way women are depicted................... 85%

TV shows contribute to violence 79%

TV violence contributes to violence in children...... 86%

Watch TV less than they did a year ago 54%

Parents monitor what their children watch 63%

Adults (with at least some college education and parents of teenage children) who think television has a negative effect on families...................................... 69%

(Source: Family Channel, Gallup Poll)

How to Take Control

Set Limits

Many families have realized the need to set limits and monitor a child's television viewing and do so by using the on/off switch. Families in control must know when to "invite" the television into their home and when not to. This control begins with a plan that you can establish with your children so that television becomes a vital part of your daily experience instead of a hazardous enemy that controls you.

In our home, we choose not to have the television on during the week on school nights. We have found that if our children don't have homework, they will spend time organizing their backpacks, rewriting class notes, reading a favorite book, or (if they are really bored!) talking with us.

On the weekends, our children choose their shows. One child might want Friday night sitcoms; another might choose cartoons on Saturday morning; still another child might choose to watch the televised football game. By limiting what they watch each day and each week, they have discovered other activities that are more satisfying than being entertained by the TV—reading, interacting with friends, playing games, practicing the piano or guitar, and ironing clothes for school.

As you limit TV in your home, be firm on the amount of time your child can watch. You might start with "only one hour on school days," then let the TV stay off until the weekend. Let us warn you: Your child will not be delighted with this new choice to limit TV viewing. In fact, to a child who has had a steady diet of television, there will be some withdrawal symptoms such as anger, temper tantrums, and moodiness. But if you provide alternatives to fill his or her time such as board games, library books, art supplies, and family conversation—and participate with them—they will get used to a new "habit" and to the new family rules.

Carefully Choose the Shows

Before you allow the television set to be turned on, look through the published television guide and decide on a specific show—together. This selection is important as you carefully weigh the choices among the offerings. In our family with five members, we often have to vote on shows; if three members vote on a show, the other members will select their favorite the next evening. An important rule for all parents is that after you watch the selected show, turn off the television, and talk about it with your child.

One of the greatest temptations in most families, ours included, is to let the set continue to run just to see "what is on next." We handle this by getting in the habit of turning off the set after a show has been viewed. This careful selection of programs has helped our children acquire a taste for quality programming as they mature, and it hopefully will keep them from developing an addiction for TV.

Develop Your Own Family Standards for Television

As you regain control of the media's influence in your home, it is important to develop some family standards. The following standards are what we use for television, but you can modify these to include any form of media, including movies, music and videos.

➤ Is the program something your child would choose to watch or is it just blaring noise?
➤ How much time has your child spent watching TV today? This week?
➤ If your child weren't watching TV, would he or she be engaged in a more productive activity such as exercise, reading, or interacting with friends?
➤ Does the show promote the Christian values that you believe in or that you are teaching your child?
➤ Does the program portray violence or graphic sexual activity? Does it focus negatively upon races? Does it treat all people equally or is one race or sex in control?
➤ Is the show something your child would choose to watch, or is it a habit at this time of day?
➤ Is there a program on public television at this time that might be educational for the child?
➤ Is your child old enough to understand that the program is make-believe or not real?
➤ Is the program uplifting, educational, or entertaining or does it make you depressed and dull?
➤ Does the show promote your Christian family values?
➤ Are slang terms or offensive language used on the show something that might be picked up by your child?

Read these questions to your children; then select a television show they enjoy and see how it measures up. Sometimes children can make wise decisions if they know the rules.

Do Not Use Television as a Baby-sitter

We have to admit our own guilt in turning on the television set for those creative children's programs when our three were very young. "Go watch 'Sesame Street,'" or "'Mr. Rogers' is on," we would say. But we became aware that using this object to entertain or baby-sit children is not healthy for developing personalities, and this habit changed quickly.

When a child views show after show, he is not required to think; and the mind suffers. When a child sits and meditates on super heroes, he is not required to move; and the body suffers. And when a child watches violence on the set, he becomes numb emotionally; and the spirit suffers.

Television viewing is related to obesity, violence, and aggressive behavior. The values children receive influence what children feel about drugs and alcohol, promiscuity, and racial stereotypes. Do you want this type of influence guiding your children? Probably not.

Talk About What You See

The key for responsible viewing lies in the hands of the home audience. Being with your children as they watch certain programs is vital for intelligent television viewing. Children may accept what they see at face value, and violence may not be interpreted by some children as acting. Caring adults must assist children in interpreting what they watch.

Talking with your children about the show and asking questions for open discussion are keys to regaining control of the television. Ask them if the actor talks the way your family is allowed to talk in your home. Ask if the program is praising the "good guy" or the "bad guy." Remember, even fantasy cartoons can be brutal and violent!

Discuss pretending and how the actors are not really living this way. If you have young children, let them dress up in old clothes and explain that they are pretending—just like on TV.

This communication is especially important when viewing the commercials. Whether it is the latest cereal or the newest form of makeup, you can help your children see through the glamour and focus on the reality of the product described. Talk about the practicality of the item. If it is a food, question its nutritional value. Is the food appealing because it tastes good or because it has a special game inside? By sticking with your children from time to time while they are in front of the set, you can help them become discerning viewers.

Just when you think you can trust your child to watch decent TV programs, they become adolescents. If you have teenagers, you must continue to view certain programs with your child. Watch MTV, "Beavis and Butt-head," "The Simpsons" and other popular programs that most teens view. What values do they talk about? What type of language is used? Do they depict sex, love, and relationships in an exaggerated manner, implying that "everyone's doing it"? Do they promote the personal standards that are in your home? Do they ridicule a certain sex or race? In defense of these favorite shows, teens may tell you, "Hey, get a life. It's just TV." But a steady diet of the wrong values is bound to be internalized by your teen.

Several years ago, after watching MTV in our presence for a few minutes, our teens became so embarrassed that "Mom and Dad were hearing this 'stuff'" that they turned the set off and went to their rooms to read. Make sure the "stuff" that is being said and shown in your home from the TV is worthy to enter.

Turn It Off

What is most important is to not ever hesitate to turn the television show off if the show is not appropriate or if it is offensive to your family. So many parents say, "We watched the most gruesome movie last night. We can't believe the station would run that during prime time when children are up." The viewer has ultimate control over the television. When this excellent means of communication has crossed the line and becomes offensive, there is only one way to stop it—turn it *off*.

Marie told us that she does not allow violent television programs or cartoons to "enter" their home. "The kids know that I am firm about this—no violence," she said. "They don't even try to talk me into one show. This is one thing I believe in and will not waver."

Parents who control what is going on in the home do make rules and stand firm when someone tries to challenge these rules, as Marie does. Decide what is important in your home, what types of television shows you want your children to view, and stand firm as you say no should anyone test your family rules.

Other Areas of Concern

The average child sees more than twenty thousand commercials during the thirteen hundred to fourteen hundred hours of television viewed each year. Advertisers spend roughly $700 million a year to make sure that their sales pitches reach most children. More than 60 percent of the commercials are for sugared cereal, candy, fatty foods, and toys, and the top TV advertisers are corporations that aim all or most of their sales efforts at our children.[3]

Must We Be Taken in by Commercials?

If you are a parent of teenagers, you need to take an even more careful look at the commercials. The ones aimed at this vulnerable age group include beer commercials that portray healthy athletes and gorgeous female models laughing and drinking at bars; makeup commercials that claim their product will "change your looks;" diet products that make losing weight a breeze, and more.

You may see the hazards in these commercials, but teens view these as reality—drinking beer will make you attractive to the opposite sex; the right makeup will help you look like that fameous TV model; and "safe" diet pillshelp you stay slim.

Talk with your child and your teen about commercials on television, and let him know the reality. Tell him how alcohol will numb his senses, how the models on television represent a fraction of our population, and how diet pills can make them very ill and injure their good health. If advertisers are going to continue to portray an unreal society, parents must set their children straight about the truth in advertising.

If you feel that an advertisement is misleading to your family, write down the product information and when it was shown. Let your Better Business Bureau have this information along with your views, or send it to:

Children's Advertising Review Unit
Council of Better Business Bureaus, Inc.
845 Third Avenue
New York, NY 10022

Violence on Television

In a recent Gallup poll, 80 percent of the people surveyed said that there is too much violence on television. One frightening study said that by the time a child has finished elementary school, he or she will have witnessed an estimated eight thousand murders and one hundred thousand acts of violence. A leading social scientist claims that TV programming is to blame for 10 percent of the violent crimes in America today. [4] About three thousand studies have been done during the past four decades examining TV violence. Most researchers agree: Violence does hurt.

Knowing that our impressionable children and teens can be affected by programs that represent out-of-control, hostile behavior, why are they still shown on TV? The response is simple—the violent shows sell.

Like everything else shown on television, the violence on programs is exaggerated. It presents a much higher rate of crime than in our world today, and the acts of violence on television are premeditated, stemming from greed, jealousy, and revenge. TV violence introduces our children to a fantasy world where shootings, stabbings, car chases, and bombings are almost cheered and revered. You can observe a group of elementary-aged children watch a car chase in a Saturday morning cartoon. Every time the car hits a person or object, you will hear the kids clap and cheer for the driver.

What About MTV?

MTV is the first television network designed specifically to say to young people, "We've got the answers to the problems that you have regarding intimacy and identity." The whole channel was set up with that in mind, and the people who designed it knew exactly what they were doing. For instance, when they set up the VJs, which are the video equivalent of disc jockeys, they said, "Let's have them in a very personal environment, kind of like a family room. We'll dress them informally and make it seem live, so that the individual teenage viewer watching will feel like he or she is developing a relationship—an intimacy—with a VJ as a friend."[5]

Many teenagers whose parents are not communicating with them in the home will learn about life, love, and relationships from MTV. The discerning parent needs to carefully watch MTV and see if the values conveyed are going to help or hurt their teenager. If you disagree with the MTV message as we do, do not let it come in your home. One parent told us, "But my kids will hate me, scream, and yell if I ban MTV from our home." The sad note here is that parents who are afraid to stand up to their children on something like MTV are probably weak in other areas as well. This is not easy, but you can draw the line.

What Else Can Parents Do About TV?

You do not have to let violent programs or networks like MTV cross the boundary in your family. If turning the TV off does not end the problem, then more aggressive steps might be needed. There are many consumer-friendly groups across the nation that monitor violent acts in TV programs and movies. These watchdog groups care about the consumers—consumers buy products and spend money. If the consumers are not happy and are turning off the shows, advertisements don't reach the audience intended. While we are waiting for dramatic changes to happen in television programs today, you can voice your opinion in different ways:

> Contact your local Parent-Teacher Association or School Advisory Committee, and let them know how you feel about inappropriate television shows.
> Meet with other concerned parents, and write letters to your congressman or senator as they vote on bills that legislate such programming. Let them know the facts and how you, as voters, regard such shows.
> Call the ABC hotline number (1-800-213-6222), and let them hear your opinion. This line monitors the violence ABC airs.
> Get a program lock-out device from your cable franchise. Most companies offer these free.
> Write to the National Coalition on Television Violence for its rating of video game violence: (P. O. Box 2157, Champaign, IL 61825.)
> Write to Action for Children's Television (ACT, 20 University Road, Cambridge, MA 02138). This has been a leading public interest group for correct and appropriate programming for children.

While some people say that when they throw away the television set they begin to rediscover the family, you might not have to go to that extreme. With careful rules in your home, cautious program selections and moderation in viewing, families can enjoy a discriminating use of the television set and still maintain the values of a Christian family.

But What About Movies and Videos?

It is sad that there are so few family-oriented movies being released today. But a glance at the movie section in your newspaper will confirm that there are rarely G-rated movies. Knowing this, parents must be more careful about movie selectio, especially when movies advertised during children's television shows are often PG or PG13. The same rules that apply to screening television shows apply to choosing movies and videos—make selections for your child very carefully.

Using the Family Standards for Television on page 230, apply these guides to the movies or videos your child wants to see. A universal rating system has been developed using codes to guide parents in this selection. Check this rating to see if the program is age-appropriate and if it is consistent with the Christian values you are teaching.

Current Rating for Movies

G - General audience, suitable for all ages.

PG - Parent discretion.

PG13 - Not suitable for children under 13; parent should view first

R - Restricted; viewers under 17 must be accompanied by an adult

NC17 - Must be 17 or older to view this movie.

In many cases a PG movie may be appropriate for an older child—*if* you preview it ahead of time. Keep in mind that your pastor did not design these ratings! Many times offensive words are used in PG movies that may surprise you and intrigue a young, impressionable child.

Choosing Appropriate Music for Your Child

For some children and most teens, music is their world. Although the music industry offers such Christian artists such as Amy Grant and Michael W. Smith, many teens are still attracted to music filled with profanity, perverted thoughts, and suggestions of alternative lifestyles. Much of rap music places women in an inferior role, and if you listen carefully, some of the most popular rock groups speak favorably of drugs, alcohol, sexual involvement, and even suicide. Where do parents draw the line?

Check the Content Before Purchasing

Although it is not mandatory in the record industry, music that may have questionable lyrics is usually marked with a label stating "Parental Advisory-Explicit Lyrics." While children and teens are still allowed to purchase this music, it does serve as a red flag for the parent. One national music and video chain has taken this one step further and labels music that is inappropriate for teens with "Must be 18 or older to buy this item. ID required."

Go with your child to make these purchases. Ask the sales people to guide you as your child or teen makes selections, and use discretion—if you are not sure of a CD or tape's content, do not purchase it until you are.

What About Older Teens?

It is difficult to give absolutes to older teens when they control the radio stations and tape or CD players in their cars. At this point in a child's life, parents are no longer present to monitor music with them; the choices they make are now their own. While this transition may be difficult, you will need to trust that your teen will make sound judgments while away from home; and continue talking with your teen about your family's morals and values.

While it is normal for older teens to begin to question the values they grew up with at this age of independence, we firmly believe that if the platform of faith is strong, they will always have high morals to fall back on. Strong Christian families bring about strong Christian families.

Enjoy some of their music, even if you must wear ear plugs! If your older teens have the stereos on in their rooms, go in and join them for a while. Talk about some of the lyrics with them, if they are inappropriate. Make them aware of what they are "feeding" their mind, and talk about the offensive values this music is conveying. Teens may challenge you by saying, "The lyrics don't matter; it is the music that is important." But your open discussion will give them food for thought when they hear the piece again.

One method of getting teens to think about the lyrics they listen to is to ask them, "Would you want your child or younger sister (or brother) to listen to these words?" This one sentence can put everything into perspective. Even though they may feel the lyrics are acceptable and harmless to them, they often admit that they would *never* let their sibling or child hear the same words. Often this one sentence opens the teen's mind in a way nothing else can.

Occasionally we have "filed," or thrown in the garbage, CDs and tapes that were not fitting for our children. We have never considered this a waste of money; rather we feel that allowing our children to listen to undesirable lyrics is a waste of their mind and values. Again, parents must take control of this area if they are to reclaim the family.

Then Someone Invented Video Games

We admit that our children once were addicted to video games—before we began to see the damage they could cause *if* no limits were set. One summer vacation we took the small TV and a portable video game to the mountain cabin. We set these up in one of the bedrooms so the "kids could play when they got tired." Were we wrong! The first day of our vacation, they played the game when they woke up, missed lunch because they wanted "their turn," and refused to participate in family activities such as trail hikes so they could continue. Even in the wee hours of the morning, we heard the repetitive sounds of the video game in the next room.

After a day of watching three healthy children lying on the floor like couch potatoes, hypnotized to this animated screen, we unplugged it and locked it in our car. The rest of vacation was spent climbing mountains, fishing in the trout-filled lake, and hunting for waterfalls.

When we returned home, we talked about the much-loved video game set and established limits for them, such as:

➤ Video games are allowed only on weekends during the school year.
➤ You may only play for thirty minutes each day.
➤ If your grades are down, there are no video games.
➤ If we see the video game creating conflict in a family relationship, it will go in the closet.

We must be honest at this point and tell you that our popular video game is still sitting at the top of the hall closet as we write this book! Once our children got into the game they were playing, they could not handle the limits we imposed. This expensive "child's toy" created more conflict in our family than one could realize.

No one can decide what is right for your family but you. Observe your children as they engage in this game. Are they so absorbed in this that they get no physical exercise? Are grades suffering? How are their peer relationships? As you begin to reclaim your family, getting in control of all forms of media, including video games, is important.

Remember, the ultimate decision as to what influences your child is up to the parent. Set up media guidelines, talk with your children about what they see and hear, teach them how to make moral choices, and stay on top of what enters your child's mind.

Family Time

1. Have a family meeting on Sunday night. Using the TV section of the newspaper, look at the upcoming television shows for the week. Have your children select the programs they want to watch. Then, using the Family Standards for Television on page 230, ask your children the questions listed. Do the programs seem appropriate? Talk with your children about opposing influences in life and how Christians are to know when to draw the line in all aspects of living in the world.

2. Take a sheet of paper, and let each family member choose favorite programs during the upcoming week. Write these down, along with the times, and post on the refrigerator. Make sure you govern how much time is spent watching these shows, and turn the television off after the show is finished. Use a common-sense approach to your family's television viewing, and continue to take control should they abuse the privilege.

3. Purchase some contemporary Christian music, and play this on the family's stereo system. Talk about the lyrics with your child or teen. Help him to understand that everyone is influenced by what they see or hear.

4. Watch Saturday morning cartoons with your children. Are they violent? Are the story lines consistent with your family's values? Even Saturday morning cartoons need to be reevaluated from time to time.

Talk with your children about the commercials aired on Saturday morning. Help them to understand that advertisers may not always be telling the truth when they advertise a sugar-coated cereal as being healthful.

Notes

1. Nancy McAlister, "The Impact of TV Makes It Medium Most Criticized for Violence" *Florida Times-Union* (Monday, Nov. 22, 1993), A-8.

2. "Do You Let MTV Answer Your Kid's Most Important Questions? An interview with Quentin J. Schultze," US Catholic (October 1990), 19.

3. "Television and the Family: Guidelines for Parents," The American Academy of Pediatrics (1991), 3.

4. "Attuned to Violence." *Florida Times-Union* (Nov. 21, 1993), E-1.

5. "Do You Let MTV Answer Your Kid's Most Important Questions? An Interview with Quentin J. Schultze," 19.

Reclaiming
Your Family

From the earliest cave-dwelling tribes to the private nuclear family dwelling of today, no human institution has been as resilient as the family. [1] The fact that you are reading this book shows that there is hope for the family today: Parents do want answers and support in how to regain control of what goes on in the home. We believe that America is on the brink of a spiritual revival of the family with this yearning for high values, commitment, and moral purpose. Instead of standing on the sidelines, Christians now stand strong against those opposing forces of society that once tore at the very heart of the family.

But even though there is hope for families today to get back in control, any parent will tell you that evaluating a family's weaknesses and taking steps to overcome these is not an easy task. As resilient as the family may be, society's forces threaten it daily. For example, the top three disciplinary problems in public schools when we were children were talking, chewing gum, and running in the halls. Now we are told that rape, robbery, and assault head the concerns for most schools throughout America.

The five greatest fears of preschoolers twenty years ago were animals, dark rooms, strangers, high places, and loud voices. What frightens our young children today? Parental divorce, nuclear war, cancer, pollution, and muggings. You can add to this list the fear of AIDS, car jacking, and home invasions. It is not easy being a child today! In our world, only the family can be that basic stabilizing force for its members. This is more important now than ever before as the family gives guidance, strength, and protection to its members.

Jesus Brings Light and Hope

"Please open the door. The darkness scares me," Ashley whispered as we turned off her light at bedtime. Then, as a ray of light from the distant hall filtered into her room, she was comforted and drifted off to sleep.

Later that evening as we carried the trash cans to the curb, the flickering light in the garage suddenly burned out. We both fumbled around in the shadowy darkness as we anchored the cans in place, then suddenly the porch floodlight came on, giving illumination to the cloudy night sky. "Thought you might need to see," Brittnye said, as she waited by the front door for us to return.

That precious ray of light! It gives us hope and strength as we stumble blindly in a darkened world and allows us to see God's way in our lives. John the Baptist came to point us to the light which was in Jesus Christ. With Jesus Christ in our home, we do not ever have to be afraid of the dark; His light shows us who we are and what we should do in our families. Once we allow the light of our Lord to guide our home, the fears that our children have and the insecurities we may have about gaining control in the home are all in vain.

You Can Reclaim Your Family

Can you reclaim your family? Let's view getting in control of what goes on in your home this way: What have you done in your life that was more significant than bringing your children into the world? Once they did not exist; now they are alive and vibrant as a true expression of your love. They came into an imperfect world needing guidance, love, affirmation, discipline, and so much more. They are dependent on you, yet independent from you. Your children hurt and laugh and create and love. In time, they too will bring more children into God's world as an expression of their love. What kind of legacy are you giving your family?

It Takes Self-denial

A few years ago we were with a group of young people in Washington, D.C. As we approached the Washington Monument, we heard the guide announcing loudly a two-hour wait to ride the elevator to the top. But with a wry smile and gleam in his eye, the guide said, "There is no waiting to go to the top if you are willing to take the stairs." There is no limit to what families can become if parents are willing to "climb the stairs" or work hard to reclaim their family. The opportunity is there for all families willing to pay the price.

Success in reclaiming the family requires a willingness to resist the temptation of the "easy way." A sound body requires that we exercise, eat nutritious foods, and conquer bad habits. A sound mind requires that we read, observe, and continually learn. A sound marriage requires that each partner goes into it with the understanding that a marriage is not fifty-fifty, but a seventy-thirty proposition in which both parties give 70 percent. Thus, having a sound family means that we must take the time to be sensitive to the needs of our children. We must provide not only for their physical needs, but for their emotional and spiritual needs as well. The path to gaining control at home is also the path of self-denial, so reclaiming the family means sacrifice, perseverance, and determination.

Some cynic once said that when the going gets tough . . . everyone leaves. That's what happened to Jesus. As the way got harder, the numbers of those who followed Him dwindled— until He finally died alone on Calvary. Yet, if Jesus had been unwilling to lay down His life, the world would never have known the love of the Father. If those early disciples had not picked up Jesus' cross and followed after Him, we still would not know about that love. And if we do not pick up the cross in our time—if we don't make those hard choices and get in control in our homes—our children and our children's children will never know the reality and benefits of a Christ-centered family.

Reclaiming your family will take some sacrifices and a bit more work as you get organized, but the rewards will be seen in a closer bond between members and children who are prepared to leave the nest and form their own families.

As you gain control of what goes on in your home, you will reshape and refocus the direction of your family. For many people, this will be a major lifestyle change, since we live in an "instant everything" society.

Several summers ago, when our niece stayed with us at the beach, we asked her to fix some hot dogs for the younger children. We watched as twelve-year-old Laura rummaged through the kitchen, opening cabinets, slamming doors. Finally she came out with her hands on her hips and in all seriousness said, "Well, I hate to break the bad news, but we can't have hot dogs for lunch today. Can you believe there is no microwave?"

Most of us are so accustomed to having quick results in all we do that we have ignored the details that produce these results. Getting in control in our families means investing our time in what is most important. Jesus said it so much better, "Where your treasure is, there will your heart be also" (Matt. 6:21). The children have our heart; our treasure is the family.

It Takes Realistic Expectations

If you think your family is going to be perfect once you gain control of what goes on in the home, perhaps you had better think again! Many times family members will falter in their responsibilities, kids' behavior will be exasperating, finances will drop, or you honestly will not "feel" as if God is with you. Families will never live happily ever after—all the time. The challenge of Hebrews 12:1 is this: "Let us run with patience the particular race that God has set before us" (TLB). This patience involves being steadfast during rough times. Remember, the Lord's time is not always our time.

It Takes Persistence

Paul offers families today strength in Acts 2:42: "They joined . . . at the apostles' teaching sessions and at the Communion services and prayer meetings" (TLB). Such persistence will motivate you to keep your family relationship strong, not to quit when situations seem tough.

Deb explains this type of persistence, one that does not let go of a child's potential, with a true story.

> Several years ago when I volunteered to be the youth Sunday School teacher at our church, the former teacher handed me the roll book with many names listed and said, "You really need to find out where these teens are. They certainly didn't come while I was teaching."
>
> I was overwhelmed by the large list of inactives, but I wanted to do my job. "I'll find each one, don't you worry," I assured the teacher with enthusiasm. And slowly, I began visiting and phoning each teenager.

I came to one inactive youth we'll call Steven. "Steven? Oh, just scratch his name off. We haven't heard from him in years," she said. *Does anyone even know where he is?* I wondered.

"Hello, Steven?" I questioned, as a young male voice answered the telephone.

"Yes, this is Steven." No enthusiasm came from the receiver.

"This is your new Sunday School teacher," I said trying to be cheerful. "I'd like to invite you to Senior Highs this week. We meet at 9:30 in the education building."

"Church? This Sunday?" His unexcited tone expressed obvious doubt, and "We'll see" was all he said.

That was not so hard, I thought. I went to class on Sunday morning and knew that my room would be filled with enthusiastic and interested teenagers. But as I looked around the youth room, I knew Steven had not come; in fact, not many of the teens in the church had responded to my personal caring.

I'll not give up, I thought. And the next week when I phoned the students on my list, I also phoned Steven.

"Steven? It's Mrs. Bruce," I said with a chuckle. "Wanted .to invite you to Sunday School again this week. Remember, the Seniors meet at 9:30."

"My Sunday School teacher again?" The teen seemed to moan as he spoke and acted a bit annoyed. But he ended again with, "We'll see."

Sunday morning came and again, no Steven. I wanted to just cross the teen's name off the roll, but the Master Shepherd had other plans. Perhaps it was providential that our Scripture lesson that morning was on the lost sheep. As I read the verse aloud to my class, I knew God was speaking to me:

"Jesus used this illustration, 'If you had a hundred sheep and one of them strayed away and was lost in the wilderness, wouldn't you leave the ninety-nine others to go and search for the lost one until you found it? And then you would joyfully carry it home on your shoulders. When you arrived you would call together your friends and neighbors to rejoice with you because your lost sheep was found'" (Luke 15:3–6, TLB).

The hundred sheep . . . were they the members on my roll? And the lost sheep . . . Steven? I had to keep finding the missing persons in my classroom, and, yes, Steven represented the one lost sheep. I was determined to find him. The persistence that now urged me on had become a divine nudge, a type of constant encouragement, and this persistence did not easily let go of the lost sheep.

Monday night I made my regular phone calls to all members on the youth roster. The next Sunday was exciting as several inactive teens were in class, but still no Steven.

I called this young man for seven weeks. Perhaps some people would have given up by then, but I know God was behind me as I made the weekly phone call once again.

"Steven, it's Debbie again," I said in a sing-song voice. Our conversations were beginning to take on a lighter note. We even got as far as talking about his new part-time job, his girl friend, and my favorite television shows.

"So, we'll see you on Sunday?" I asked hopefully after about five minutes. Again I received the same noncommittal, "We'll see."

Sunday morning came. My enthusiasm dwindled as I gathered my books and Bible together for class. This job was starting to take its toll as I diligently tried to activate the stray members. Was it worth it? As I walked into the classroom thirty minutes early and saw a lanky young man of about seventeen with a broad smile, I knew who it was.

"Steven?" It had to be him.

"Yeah," the handsome teenager replied, with a twinkle in his blue eyes. "Mrs. Bruce, I finally came so you would quit bugging me."

Bugging him? Is that what he thought? I know I blushed as I reacted to his comment, but the warmth I felt inside as God directed me to persistently rediscover one of His precious children was memorable.

Steven came regularly to the Senior class and even joined our youth choir later that month. One year later, Steven went on to college where he became a leader in the campus ministry.

Pushy? Buggy? I don't think so. I would like to call it being lovingly persistent—not willing to give up so easily on God's lost sheep.[2]

As the parents of three teens, we have learned a magnificent lesson from the Master Shepherd who is persistent enough to not scratch our name off the roll. As we face each new day with challenges that seem overwhelming, this divine persistence to believe in our children and urge them to their highest potential carries us through.

Families Who Are Gaining Control

Everyone talks about family values. Politicians use the term to get voters' attention. "We must turn back to family values," they say. And people listen! In order to reclaim the values that are dear to the people of God, parents must reevaluate the problems in their own homes and make strides to overcome these problems with some practical goal-setting and tools.

People are realizing the danger of ignoring the family. These same people can now make great strides as they determine their family's weaknesses and plan to overcome these.

Taking Control of Income

Peter and Janie are parents who are working to reclaim their family. After some stormy times with a deteriorating family business, they have finally gotten their finances straightened out and are even saving money and tithing to the church. "We were out of control in every area of our life," Peter admitted. "Janie and I worked ten hours a day, leaving the kids with my parents after school. Our evenings were spent listening to a blaring television set while we yelled at each other and the kids about homework, chores, and bills. There never seemed to be enough money or time to have any enjoyment. Life was miserable."

"Until we regrouped as a family," Janie added. "We sat down and made a list of our priorities—church, each other, the kids' activities at school, and family time. We realized that we had to focus on what was most important for our growth as Christians in order to experience peace at home."

Peter and Janie made God and church attendance a top priority, putting the family on a tight budget so they could pay off bills and give to the church, turning off the television set on school nights among other things. Janie found that if she budgeted her time at work, she could leave the business at 3:00 P.M. to pick the children up from school and stay at home with them.

"As we took steps to get more in control, we found ourselves relaxing and laughing more," Janie said. "The little things like our youngest child learning to read one night became so important to us. We're not the perfect family, but we are getting better. We just realized that we had made some wrong choices and began to make changes."

Jack, a single father of three, started a home-based business so he could be around more to raise his three children. "As an accountant I work long hours, especially during the tax season," he said. "My biggest concern was who was going to watch the kids after school. Then I decided to convert one bedroom in our home into an office. At three o'clock each day, I pick the kids up from school, then go to my home office to finish my work. I'm there for the kids, I take breaks to get them started with their homework, and I still get my work done. This has been a lifesaver for our family."

Taking Control Through Family Values

Sam and Melinda are taking control in the area of family values. "Here we are, the parents of two teenage boys, and we had never told them how we felt about premarital sex," Sam said. "We just assumed that because they were good kids that they would pick up on this. Then we read the school board was giving out condoms at Zack and Judd's high school."

"We couldn't believe this and became very nervous that our boys could be influenced in the wrong direction," Melinda said. "We have had some wonderful heart-to-heart talks lately about our family's personal standards and what Christians believe, including what we believe. Our sons needed to hear this, and we feel very comfortable with their position on abstinence."

Charles and Maggie are working on the same thing. "I never realized that parents had to teach values in the home," Maggie said. "Our children go to a Christian school and we are active in the church, but they were still exhibiting behaviors that were not right."

"We realized that our home was weak when it came to talking about personal standards and values," Charles said. "We've made a decided effort to do this, and it is making a difference in their behavior. We're just glad we caught this at an early age."

Taking Control Through Faith

Frank, the single parent of two preschoolers, is taking control of his family as he talks about God with his children. "They spend the weekends with their mother, so I am not with them when they attend church," Frank said. "One day Susannah, my five year old, looked up at me and asked if I had Jesus in my heart like Mommy does. This shocked me. My own children didn't know that I was a Christian because I never told them! I knew then that I had to share my faith with the girls and pray with them. We're so much closer now."

Sue has started to attend church with her son, Alex. "After getting up early during the week to go to work, the thought of getting up on Sunday morning was painful," Sue admitted. "But with my husband working as a pilot on weekends, I realized that I'm all Alex has. If I don't take him to Sunday School and church, he will never have a Christian heritage to lean on when he is older. I remember my parents going to church with me as a child, and it gave me so much strength. I want to do the same for my son."

Taking Control Through Discipline

Juanita, the mother of twin teenage boys, holds family meetings to focus on discipline. "My husband died a year ago, and I haven't wanted to put any pressure on the boys," she said. "But they have become mouthy and arrogant. We are now holding weekly meetings to talk over the rules and restrictions. I can't worry about hurting their feelings; it would hurt them a lot worse if I didn't discipline them."

Pete and Carla also have tightened up on their discipline at home. "It is so difficult when both parents work full time," Carla said. "I will come home and almost ignore the bad behavior or sassy language simply because I'm too tired to deal with this. But we know that's the wrong approach."

"We've had to establish some firm rules with the kids recently and we let them know the consequences," Pete said. "Carla and I made a pact that no matter how tired we are, these kids will come first. The kids sense that we are firmer, and their behavior is getting more respectful."

Taking Control Through Communication

Another family taking control could not communicate before. "We both came from homes that never encouraged openness or asking questions," Julia said. "So we have raised our children the same way, until we overheard our oldest daughter ask a friend if she had ever tried drugs. I immediately told Erika that she could talk to me anytime about drugs, and she said, 'But we've never talked before.'"

"Julia and I realized then that family discussions had to become part of our home or we were going to be faced with some heavy problems later on," Richard said. "We began to comment on commercials we heard on the radio or TV, asked the children questions about news stories, and gave our opinion openly. This was not easy for us! But the kids cannot stop asking questions now. I just wish we had started this sooner."

"Jason had become such a loner in his teen years," Mary, a single parent, said. "It seemed as if we did not have anything in common. But it also concerned me that our relationship was stilted because we never really talked or laughed together."

"We have been going out to dinner once a week after work for our mother-son 'bonding night,'" she continued. "You would be amazed at how this has forced us to communicate. As we sit across the table from each other, we have no choice but to talk. I've learned so much about my only son lately, and I hope he feels the same way."

Taking Control of Time

Connie and Bill, the parents of four young children, never had enough time to have fun. "Can you believe that all we did was work and take care of our children?" Connie said. "I spent the days running carpools, cooking, and going to volunteer meetings in the community, and Bill stayed late at his law office. He would come home after the kids were in bed, and by then I would be so exhausted that often I just fell asleep in the chair."

"It hit us one day that our kids weren't really experiencing what a real family was," Bill said. "I started to take off earlier from work so I could eat with Connie and the kids. Weekends became family time, and we started planning outings to enjoy our children. Here we had financial resources but made no time to enjoy this with our children. Our family was so incomplete, but we now see some hope."

Mark, father of ten-year-old Annie, said, "Two years ago, I could give you anything except time. I was at the peak of my career, traveled Monday through Friday, then spent the weekends sitting in my recliner watching sports, while Rebecca did church and scouting activities with Annie."

"One Saturday Annie had her best friend over. The child stared at me for a long time and then asked Annie, 'Who is that man in your house?'" Mark continued. "It hit me that I could never recapture the time I was gone; I didn't even know my only daughter's friends. I guess I'm getting sentimental in my old age, but I want to be with my family. I want to know my wife and daughter, and I want them to know that this dad cares. I've reworked my schedule so that I'm now home three full days each week—days we spend together."

Taking Control of Television

"I could not stand television," Lilli said. "I would walk in the house and there my kids were, staring at that set. I called their names, and they ignored me. It's as if they were in a trance. But I realized that I had allowed the television to take over my home.

"It was just easier to turn on the TV than to deal with three kids each afternoon," she continued. "But that's changed. We have a new policy of only one program on school nights. We interact more now. The kids are responsive to me and look at me when I speak. The TV was really disrupting our home."

Kip and Bettye, parents of two teenagers, agree that television can disrupt families. "Our teens were getting a steady diet of MTV—day and night," Kip said. "We wanted to tell them no, but we didn't want any power struggles with them."

Bettye added: "One night I walked into the den and heard a commercial for condoms. I could not believe my ears, but it was true. We had a long talk that night and asserted our parental privilege—Mom and Dad are in charge of the home. We feel MTV is wrong for our kids, and it's okay to turn the set off. Oh, they were angry with us for several days, but things are getting better now. Even their language, behavior, and dress does not seem as strange as it did."

Parents Are Taking Charge of the Family

So many families are taking control—with communication like Julia and Richard, with faith talks like Frank and his girls, with family meetings and more discipline like Juanita, with ordered priorities like Peter and Janie, with church attendance as a family like Sue, with television like Kip and Bettye, and more. And parents who are reclaiming the family are realizing that taking control is not always easy; it takes time, energy, and some lifestyle changes. But just as God made the choice to give His life for us—knowing that this sacrifice would result in new life for you and me—parents must make drastic choices and sacrifices in the family in order to give their children hope and security in a changing world.

While these are tough times for many families throughout the country, the problems must be viewed as challenges, not barriers. Families are getting in control of what goes on in the home with a new determination and optimism, showing that there is hope even in times of peril.

Remember, if we do not talk about personal standards and morals, who will? If we do not communicate and discipline our children, who will? If we do not screen television programs, who will? And if we do not tell our children about the love of Jesus Christ, who will? Jesus said, "If anyone wishes to come after me, let him deny himself and take up his cross, and follow Me" (Mark 8:34). This is the ultimate call to families across the globe today—self-denial and commitment. Can He count on you?

We believe that deep within the hearts of most Americans today is an intense yearning for deeper commitment, purpose, and the highest family values. Some may deny it; others seek it in the wrong places. But we know that there is hope for the family, and there is help. It is found in the person of Jesus Christ for He alone has the authority and power to heal all who ask. Trust in Him today as you reclaim your family!

Notes

1. Mary Miller Pedersen, "The Family: Symbol of God's Covenant Love," *The Catholic World* (July/August 1993), 190.

2. Robert Bruce and Debra Fulghum Bruce, *Growing a Great Sunday School Class* (Nashville: Abingdon, 1994), Paraphrased, 31.